D1372579

POP CULTURE

American Life and Television from I Love Lucy to Mad Men

MARK MUSSARI

Cavendish
Square

New York

For Eleanor—my coconspirator in all things television.

Published in 2014 by Cavendish Square Publishing, LLC
303 Park Avenue South, Suite 1247, New York, NY 10010

Copyright © 2014 by Cavendish Square Publishing, LLC

First Edition

CPSIA Compliance Information: Batch #WS13CSQ

All websites were available and accurate when this book was sent to press.

Library of Congress Cataloging-in-Publication Data

Mussari, Mark.. • American life and television from I Love Lucy to Mad Men / Mark Mussari.
p. cm. — (Pop culture). • Summary:"Provides a comprehensive look at the history of television in America"—Provided by publisher.
Includes bibliographical references and index.
ISBN 978-1-60870-923-6 (hardcover)—ISBN 978-1-62712-123-1 (paperback)—
ISBN 978-1-60870-928-1 (ebook)
1. Television programs—United States—History.
2. Television broadcasting—United States—History. I. Title.
PN1992.3.U5M873 2013. • 791.450973—dc23. • 2011036023

Series Consultant: Mark Mussari • Art Director: Anahid Hamparian
Series Designer: Alicia Mikles • Photo research by Lindsay Aveilhe

The photographs in this book are used by permission and through the courtesy of:

Cover photo courtesy of AMC/The Kobal Collection and CBS-TV/The Kobal Collection.
Pictorial Press Ltd/Alamy: p. 5; Bettmann/Corbis: p. 8; CBS-TV/The Kobal Collection: p. 14; John Springer Collection/Corbis: p. 16; Time & Life Pictures/Getty Images: p. 20; CBS Photo Archive/Getty Images: p. 24, 27; AF archive/Alamy: p. 29; Thomas/Spelling/The Kobal Collection: p. 32; Pictorial Press Ltd/Alamy: p. 33; Time & Life Pictures/Getty Images: p. 36; Steven Clevenger/Getty Images: p. 38; CBS Photo Archive/Getty Images: p. 41; Pictorial Press Ltd/Alamy: p. 43; NBCU Photo Bank/AP Images: p. 48; NBC Television/Getty Images: p. 49; MPI/Getty Images: p. 52; Alice S. Hall/NBCU Photo Bank/AP Images: p. 57; Everett Collection: p. 59; Universal TV/20th Century Fox TV/Klasky-Scupo/Album/Newscom: p. 63; Court POOL/ZUMA Press/Newscom: p. 66; AF archive/Alamy: p. 71, 75, 78; Reuters/Corbis: p. 80;Getty Images: p. 84; Getty Images: p. 87; AMC/Everett Collection: p. 89; Moviestore collection Ltd/Alamy: p. 94; Charles Dharapak; AP Photo: p. 96.

Printed in the United States of America

Contents

INTRODUCTION 5

1. 1950s: TELEVISION'S GOLDEN AGE 7

2. 1960s: IN LIVING COLOR 21

3. 1970s: CHANGING VALUES—
   CHANGING TIMES 39

4. 1980s: EXPANDING HORIZONS 51

5. 1990s: SETTING NEW STANDARDS 65

6. 2000s: REALITY AND REALITY TV
   IN THE FIRST DECADE 81

CONCLUSION 99

NOTES 100

FURTHER INFORMATION 103

BIBLIOGRAPHY 105

INDEX 106

In the early 1950s, only about half of all American homes had a television set. Families would gather around the set at night, and sometimes even invite in their neighbors who could not afford a television of their own.

Introduction

IT'S DIFFICULT TO IMAGINE A WORLD without television. Yet even in the years immediately following World War II (1939–1945), most Americans did not own televisions. The technology was new and sets were expensive. In fact, only 0.5 percent of households had television sets in 1946. By 1954 that number had jumped to 55.7 percent, and it skyrocketed to 90 percent in 1962. Television became an integral and pervasive part of American culture. Today, it is common for most households to own more than one television.

Television is a powerful cultural medium for a number of reasons. First and foremost, it has bought profound and historic moments into viewers' homes, from a man landing on the moon to an athlete winning a gold medal at the Olympics to presidential inaugurations.

Second, television reaches across all segments of society—rich and poor, young and old, urban and rural, and all ethnicities and races. People from diverse backgrounds can enjoy the same situation comedy (commonly known as a sitcom), drama series, or talk show, uniting them in a shared cultural experience.

Third, television connects people globally by enabling them to view news and entertainment programs from different countries. Almost every country in the world has at least one broadcasting network, and many countries show television programs from other parts of the world. The television phenomenon *American Idol* actually began in the UK, but was called *Pop Idol*. There have been versions of *Idol* in Bulgaria, Turkey, Norway, and Vietnam.

Since the 1950s, television has been an integral part of popular culture. Popular television programming reflects the culture we live in and, at the same time, influences attitudes, styles, and values. From *I Love Lucy* to *The Twilight Zone*, from *The Carol Burnett Show* to *Friends*, from *Dragnet* to *Mad Men*—television programs have affected our collective consciousness. They have entertained us and moved us in ways that no other medium could.

Even though television is sometimes called "the boob tube" and "the idiot box," television programs can also make us think about important issues and ideas. For better or worse, television has helped make many of us who we are today—both as people and as nations.

THE 1950s:

Television's Golden Age

IN THE UNITED STATES, THE ERA FOLLOWING World War II was a time of great expansion and growth. Many soldiers returned home from war and entered the workforce. The economy boomed and families moved out of cities and into newly formed suburbs—with new schools, new roads, and new shopping centers. The automobile became an essential part of American life. Gasoline was cheap, and new highways connected cities and states, making travel easier than ever before.

American citizens began taking a greater interest in national affairs. Television, like much of popular culture, played a major role in connecting Americans from all walks of life. The powerful visual impact of televised news programs slowly drew families away from gathering around the radio for news and information, and influential broadcast journalists like Edward R. Murrow became household names.

Because of a large growth in population during the late 1940s and 1950s, the generation known as the "baby boomers" was the first to be raised sitting directly in front of this new and influential medium. Decades would pass before the immense power of television became clear.

BEGINNINGS—THE 1940S

Looking at the limited television schedules throughout the mid–1940s, one would assume that people watched mostly sports and news. Programs were transmitted in black and white, as color television sets did not yet exist. Popular shows included *Gillette Cavalcade of Sports* (sponsored by the razor-making company Gillette), *Boxing from Jamaica Arena*, and *Sports from Madison Square Garden*. An occasional entertainment program popped up. For example, *Broadway Preview* offered sneak previews of upcoming Broadway plays. *Faraway Hill*, the first ongoing soap opera, debuted in October 1946.

That same year *Kraft Television Theater* debuted on NBC. It was the first time that a drama series was not only sponsored by a major company (Kraft) but was also produced by an agency outside the network. At the time, networks usually produced their own shows, including dramas. Perhaps even more importantly, Kraft had found a good place to advertise one of its products: cheese! The Kraft brand became a huge success, thanks to two straight weeks of heavy advertising.

Television as a powerful advertising tool had truly been born. Not only was television an unparalleled means of mass communication, but it was also becoming the greatest advertising medium in the world. Television's ability to reach such a wide audience had a profound and lasting effect on its influence on popular culture. The children now known as the baby boomers were the first generation to be affected by the influential power of television.

Early television shows such as the *Texaco Star Theater* often featured vaudeville-like routines: this one features Milton Berle and Ethel Merman.

COMMERCIAL BEGINNINGS

When did the first television commercial air? On July 1, 1941, Bulova Watch Company ran a paid advertisement—costing $9—during a televised baseball game between the Brooklyn Dodgers and the Philadelphia Phillies. During the commercial, a silhouetted map of the United States appeared with the slogan: "America Runs on Bulova Time." Since then, commercials have undoubtedly been taking up a lot of our time.

THE FLOODGATES OPEN

In 1947, the U.S. government agency known as the FCC (the Federal Communications Commission) approved full-scale, commercial television broadcasting in black-and-white, in effect opening the door for new television stations around the country. Before this decision, government regulation limited transmission of television signals. Convinced that television would become a national sensation, stations immediately began to plan programming to fill the airwaves.

In *Watching TV: Six Decades of American Television*, Harry Castleman and Walter J. Podrazik state, "The expansion of television during the first nine months of 1948 was nothing short of miraculous." At the time, there were four major television networks: ABC, CBS, NBC, and the short-lived DuMont network.

VARIETY PROGRAMS

Two of television's early successes were variety programs: *Texaco Star Theater*, starring the irrepressible comedian Milton Berle, and Ed Sullivan's *The Toast of the Town* (later to be known as *The Ed Sullivan Show*).

Texaco Star Theater was one of television's first commercial hits and became the number one rated show in 1950–1951. Berle was a comedian of the vaudeville era—a theater genre known for its broad variety of performers. Berle's variety show relied heavily on sketches, short comedy routines in which he often appeared with guest stars. This format would have a lasting effect on television comedy, defining the format for such variety shows as *The Carol Burnett Show*, *Saturday Night Live*, and *In Living Color*.

Ed Sullivan was a former sportswriter and entertainment journalist who became a television host on *The Toast of the Town*. Sullivan's show also used a vaudeville format by presenting many different acts—from singers to comedians to circus performers to puppets. *The Toast of the Town* was a broad potpourri of talent rolled into one hour. Sullivan's show was geared toward the entire family, and guests included both established stars and younger performers. Sullivan had perfected this format when he introduced Elvis Presley to the American viewing audience in 1956.

Berle and Sullivan offered just what people were looking for at the end of their workday. People needed to relax and wanted to be entertained. Families could gather around the television set and enjoy both of these shows. As the radio had done in previous years, the television initially drew families together.

Throughout the 1950s, variety shows presented a winning combination of comedy and music. The hosts of these popular variety programs included established stars such as singer Perry Como and comedians Red Skelton and Garry Moore. In 1951 singer Dinah Shore became the first woman to host her own variety series, sponsored by Chevrolet. Meanwhile, *Walt Disney Presents* featured different shows—either live-action or animated—from Walt Disney Productions each week.

VARIETY'S INNOVATORS

Two of TV's most clever creators of variety were Sid Caesar and Ernie Kovacs. Caesar premiered in 1950 with *Your Show of Shows*, a ninety-minute blend of music and comedy. Imogene Coca, who co-starred with Caesar, would go on to have her own variety series in 1954. Employing free-form ad-libbing and sarcasm, Ernie Kovacs introduced viewers to an edgier, more experimental, more visual form of variety that would influence such shows as *Monty Python's Flying Circus* and *Saturday Night Live*.

TV FAMILIES IN THE 1950s

Today we are accustomed to homes in which, if there are two parents, both parents work and take part in raising children and running a house. In the 1950s, especially among white, middle-class families, husbands usually went to work and most—though not all—wives stayed home, devoting their time to raising children and keeping house. The booming economy allowed most families to function on one income. Also, sexism and limited professional options kept many women from entering certain segments of the workforce.

SITCOMS

This traditional view of the family was strongly represented on television, especially in the half-hour programs known as sitcoms. The decade's most popular sitcoms included *Father Knows Best, Leave It to Beaver,* and *The Adventures of Ozzie and Harriet.* In all these shows, parents are presented as moral, positive, and wise figures. Fathers go to work in suits and then come home to the pristine suburbs, often to solve a problem facing the family, while mothers frequently appear in dresses—and even high heels and pearls—cooking and cleaning, while rarely raising their voices.

Though the parents of these early sitcoms may seem unrealistic today, it's easy to relate to the children. The misdeeds, lying, and troubles of the pre-teen and teenage sitcom characters reflect a typical youthful resistance to authority. On *Leave It to Beaver*, for instance, brothers Wally and Beaver often hide the truth from their parents and hang out with friends who lie and pressure the boys into situations they know will get them in trouble. None of this behavior ever reaches a level of criminality or destruction—yet it hints at the generation gap between teens and their parents in the 1950s.

WORKING WOMEN

Some early sitcoms focused on single, working women. *Our Miss Brooks* began as a dramatic radio program and premiered on television in 1952, starring Eve Arden as a high school teacher. *Private Secretary*, which premiered in 1953, featured Ann Sothern as the assistant to a theater agent. Both Arden and Sothern were film actresses who made the shift to television. *Our Miss Brooks* and *Private Secretary* paved the way for future sitcoms about single women, including *That Girl* in the 1960s and *The Mary Tyler Moore Show* in the 1970s.

I LOVE LUCY

The most well-known and influential sitcom of the 1950s is *I Love Lucy*, starring Lucille Ball and her real-life husband Desi Arnaz. Though it may seem hard to believe today, most shows in the 1950s were broadcast live as they were happening. At the insistence of Ball and Arnaz, *I Love Lucy* was the first sitcom to

I Love Lucy was the first television show to be filmed as it was broadcast, allowing the show to be rerun by the network. This was revolutionary in its time.

be filmed in front of a live studio audience, allowing the show to be broadcast in reruns. Other shows were recorded from the picture on a video monitor, and all that remains of them today are blurry tapes known as kinescopes.

I Love Lucy focused on the lives of Lucy and Ricky Ricardo. Ricky was a Cuban-born bandleader, frequently pestered by his zany, stay-at-home wife Lucy to put her into his show. Ball's comedic timing, broad delivery, and slapstick sensibilities were a huge hit with television audiences. *I Love Lucy* originally ran from 1951 to 1957, but it has survived for decades in reruns, becoming one of the most popular and influential sitcoms in television history.

CRIME BEAT

Crime fiction was another genre that found its niche with television audiences in the 1950s. *Perry Mason*, starring Raymond Burr and based on the best-selling novels of Erle Stanley Gardner, was the most popular legal drama of the decade. By the late 1950s, two of the most successful TV crime dramas were the detective series *77 Sunset Strip* and *Hawaiian Eye*. Both shows featured casts of established actors and younger stars, such as singer Connie Stevens and heartthrob Edd Byrnes, who drew in teenage viewers.

THE HONEYMOONERS

Jackie Gleason had appeared in a number of films and television shows by the time he began hosting *The Jackie Gleason Show* in 1952. While the show included singing and dancing, Gleason tucked short comedy sketches into each program, including *The Honeymooners*, one of the first television portrayals of blue-collar American workers. Gleason played Ralph Kramden, a portly bus driver who lives with his acerbic wife Alice in a shabby apartment in New York City. Audrey Meadows, whose deadpan delivery enlivened the show, played the role of Alice. Ralph's best friend is the seemingly dim-witted Ed Norton, a sewer worker, played by Art Carney.

The Honeymooners offered a gritty counterpoint to the other, sappy suburban sitcoms. It also laid the foundation for sitcoms, such as *All in the Family* and *Roseanne*, that featured dysfunctional lower- and middle-class families. After 1955, Gleason abandoned the variety portion of his program and focused solely on *The Honeymooners*.

In *The Honeyooners*, Jackie Gleason (*right*) and Art Carney (*left*) played neighbors living in a blue-collar neighborhood in New York. Contrary to most early sitcoms, which depicted well-to-do, well-adjusted families living in the suburbs, *The Honeymooners* portrayed a much less ideal existence. It was one with which many identified, both at the time and, for years, in reruns.

WINNING WESTERNS

Westerns, which were a successful genre in the movies, became increasingly popular on television during the 1950s, reflecting America's fascination with the Old West. During that time, the country had been facing expansion and wrestling with the relationships between white settlers and Native Americans. Successful TV westerns in the 1950s included *Tales of Wells Fargo*, *Maverick*, *The Rifleman*, *Life and Legend of Wyatt Earp*, *The Lone Ranger*, *Wagon Train*, and *Have Gun—Will Travel*.

CHILDREN'S PROGRAMMING

With a new generation of children growing up in front of the television, children's programming became one of the most effective ways both to entertain, and to market to, America's youth. In the 1950s, children enjoyed such popular afternoon programs as *The Mickey Mouse Club*; *Howdy Doody*; and *Kukla, Fran and Ollie*. These shows created shared experiences among young viewers and helped form the baby-boom generation's tastes and values.

THE MICKEY MOUSE CLUB

With its songs, mini-movies, and cartoons in each episode, Walt Disney's *The Mickey Mouse Club* became a national phenomenon. Cast members, who performed live on the show, were called Mouseketeers, and children all over the country wore mouse-ear hats to show their affiliation. Many of the teenage stars went on to successful film and television careers. (Although the original program ran from 1955 to 1959, a remake in the 1990s spawned the careers of Britney Spears, Justin Timberlake, Christina Aguilera, and Ryan Gosling.)

With so many programs focused on kids, television began to function like a national babysitter. Children came home from school and watched their favorite shows while mothers prepared dinners. Meanwhile, children and teenagers could watch *American Bandstand*, an afternoon music show originally broadcast from Philadelphia. Starring host Dick Clark, *Bandstand* featured rock-and-roll music, live performances, and dancing teenagers.

"IT'S HOWDY DOODY TIME!"

In the 1950s, children all over the United States knew the answer to the question: "What time is it, boys and girls?" Buffalo Bob was the host of *Howdy Doody*, a children's program featuring cowboy marionette Howdy Doody. *Howdy Doody* ran from 1947 until 1960 and included a Peanut Gallery, consisting of on-stage bleachers that sat about forty children. *Howdy Doody* helped lay the foundation for future children's programs like *Pee-wee's Playhouse*. The show was also one of the first to prompt mass-marketed merchandising of toys and clothing targeted directly at children.

THE DECADE IN REVIEW

The network television schedule for 1959 shows what programs were popular with audiences by the end of the decade. Sitcoms included *Leave It to Beaver*, *Father Knows Best*, *The Donna Reed Show*, and *Dennis the Menace*. In many ways, the sitcom was still in its early development—and still reflected a traditional suburban life.

Families of color were rarely seen on television in the 1950s. One major exception was singer Nat King Cole, the first African American to host his own variety series. However, even Cole—a successful and respected pop singer—had difficulty finding sponsors. His show aired for only a little over one year, from November 1956 until December 1957.

Game shows were also a staple of 1950s prime-time broadcasting. Popular evening game shows included *The Price Is Right*, *To Tell the Truth*, and *What's My Line*. In many ways, the prime-time schedule for 1959 indicates that network television was quite varied in its programming.

THE 1960s:
In Living Color

ALTHOUGH MANY PEOPLE THINK OF THE 1960s as a time of rebellion and experimentation, on television the early part of the decade closely resembled the one that came before it. The white, suburban family remained the staple of most sitcoms, reflecting the importance of the traditional family and the American dream of owning a home outside the city.

Folksy, rural sitcoms like *The Andy Griffith Show* and *The Real McCoys* also found an audience in the 1960s, possibly reflecting a yearning for a simpler time in America's history. Westerns, including the increasingly popular drama *Bonanza*, also maintained their romantic attraction for many viewers.

Yet the 1960s was undeniably a decade of change. In 1960 the two presidential candidates, Democrat John F. Kennedy and Republican Richard Nixon, held four televised debates.

The television set did more than change pop culture—it changed politics. Viewers who saw the presidential debates between candidates John F. Kennedy and Richard M. Nixon overwhelmingly felt that Kennedy had won; radio listeners felt the reverse. Since the 1960 election, the way candidates look has become at least as important as what they have to say.

Many historians feel that television gave the younger, handsome Kennedy the advantage, enabling him to win by a slim margin over Nixon. When Kennedy was assassinated just three years later in November 1963, television brought the tragedy into people's homes, uniting the country in horror and grief. The image of two-year-old John F. Kennedy Jr., saluting his father's casket became burned into the nation's collective consciousness.

In an important step for equality, the United States Congress passed the Civil Rights Act of 1964, outlawing discrimination on the basis of race, color, or national origin. This landmark legislation also influenced the depiction of minorities—especially African Americans—on television. During the decade, they would become increasingly visible in prime-time programs.

In February 1964, Ed Sullivan introduced the British rock band the Beatles on his popular Sunday-night variety hour. Almost half the country at that time—more than 70 million homes—tuned in for the event, a cultural milestone in rock-and-roll history and for the baby-boom generation.

The televised debut of the Beatles offers a joyful counterpoint to television's role in Americans' grief over President Kennedy's assassination. Both events exemplify the power of television as a medium and its role in historic and cultural events. Similarly, seeing horrific scenes of the Vietnam War on television helped sway opinion among some viewers about U.S. involvement in the war. These disturbing images changed people's attitudes toward war and helped end the selective service system (also known as "the draft") for recruiting men into the armed services. As the decade progressed, culture changed rapidly, reflecting shifting tastes and social mores—and so popular television changed as well.

IN LIVING COLOR

Television experienced a major technological change during the 1960s: more and more programs were broadcast in color. For example, *Walt Disney Presents*—a staple of Sunday night television—became *Walt Disney's Wonderful World of Color* in 1961. Although color television had existed for some time, few people owned the expensive color sets in the early 1960s. By the end of the decade, so many homes had color TVs that it would have been an oddity for a television show *not* to be seen in color!

EARLY INNOVATIONS

Two very different half-hour shows that began in 1959 and gained popularity in the new decade show innovation in television programming. One spoke to the darker side of humanity, whereas the other addressed a growing generation of teenagers.

THE TWILIGHT ZONE

In 1959, Rod Serling, a respected writer and producer of television screenplays, created *The Twilight Zone*. The original half-hour series ran until 1964. With its thought-provoking scripts and haunting narratives, it was one of the first shows to grow out of the suspense genre, mixing elements of science fiction, fantasy, and psychological thrillers. *The Twilight Zone* took storytelling to a disturbing new level that was fantastical and socially relevant. Many of the show's scripts touched on issues of greed, racism, and nationalism—addressed from a very human, personal angle.

Week after week, *The Twilight Zone*'s plots about bizarre occurrences, aliens, nuclear wars, and the inevitability of fate

In a *Twilight Zone* episode entitled "Number Twelve Looks Just Like You," actress and model Suzy Parker plays a young woman who does not want to undergo a mandatory operation that will make her look beautiful but take away her individuality. Under the guise of science fiction, Rod Serling frequently tackled social issues such as this one on conformity.

spoke to the nation's fears and longings. The show also touched people on a personal, psychological level—probably the greatest reason for its enduring popularity. It remains one of the most respected and influential shows ever produced.

DOBIE GILLIS

The Many Loves of Dobie Gillis first aired in 1959, offering a youthful take on the sitcom. Instead of a suburban family, the show revolved around a group of teenagers: Dobie Gillis, his beatnik friend Maynard G. Krebs, and their gal-pal Zelda Gilroy. It was the first sitcom to focus on teens instead of family life.

The structure of *Dobie Gillis* strayed from the conventional sitcom. At times, Dobie broke the "fourth wall." Instead of speaking only to the other characters in the show, Dobie would turn to the camera and speak directly to the viewer. Comedian George Burns had pioneered this effect on *The George Burns and Gracie Allen Show*, which debuted in 1950.

ADULT CARTOON?

That's what *TV Guide* called *The Flintstones* when it debuted on prime time in 1960. Created by William Hanna and Joseph Barbera, the animated sitcom is set in prehistoric times and appears loosely based on *The Honeymooners*. Fred Flintstone even resembled the portly Jackie Gleason. The show became an instant success, enjoyed by children and adults. In 1962, Hanna-Barbera produced another animated sitcom, *The Jetsons*, focusing on a futuristic space-age family and their robot maid. *The Flintstones* and *The Jetsons* paved the way for other adult cartoons, such as *The Simpsons* in the 1980s, *South Park* in the 1990s, and *Family Guy* in the first decade of the twenty-first century.

SITCOMS

The Andy Griffith Show arrived in 1960—a gentle comedy about widowed sheriff Andy Taylor who lived with his Aunt Bee and his son Opie (played by Ron Howard). *The Beverly Hillbillies* told the story of the Clampetts, a backwoods family who become millionaires and move to Beverly Hills, California. The show remained so popular it inspired a feature-length film in 1993. Other successful 1960s sitcoms with rural settings included *Petticoat Junction*, *Green Acres*, and *Mayberry RFD*. Large parts of the United States were still rural, and these shows especially appealed to that population.

Two of the decade's most successful sitcoms had magic on their side. *Bewitched* starred Elizabeth Montgomery as a witch who marries a mortal man and tries to survive life in suburbia without using magic. *I Dream of Jeannie* featured Barbara Eden as a genie who lives in a bottle in the home of her "master," an astronaut. Both sitcoms feature women in traditional or even subservient roles with powers that make them stronger than their male counterparts.

Following in the footsteps of earlier shows about single, working women, *That Girl*—starring Marlo Thomas—premiered in 1966. Thomas played Ann Marie, a struggling actress in New York. Although she becomes engaged to her longtime boyfriend in the final season (1970–1971), Thomas insisted that the character not marry. For TV, *That Girl* was an early step toward the growing feminist movement of the 1960s.

In 1968, African American actress Diahann Carroll starred as a widowed nurse raising a child alone in *Julia*, the first sitcom with a black lead character. While the show ran for two years, television critics thought it was too saccharine and—in many ways—too similar to other average sitcoms on television. Some black critics faulted the show for its absence of a strong male lead.

In 1969, ABC premiered *The Brady Bunch*, a sitcom about a widow with three young girls who marries a widower with three young boys. Many baby boomers born in the 1960s grew up with the show, which aired for five years. Despite its sappy plots and over-the-top acting, the show became a cultural touchstone for many viewers.

SOPHISTICATED SITCOM

One of television's most admired sitcoms arrived in 1961: *The Dick Van Dyke Show*. Created by Carl Reiner, who had cowritten and starred in Sid Caesar's *Your Show of Shows*, a 1950s variety show, the sitcom revolved around the life of TV comedy writer Rob Petrie (Van Dyke). It also introduced the two-set format typical of many modern sitcoms: home and work.

While most 1950s and 1960s sitcoms centered around the home, as if work did not exist, *The Dick Van Dyke Show* gave at least equal weight to the workplace, a formula that has lasted into the present in popular shows such as *30 Rock*.

At work, Rob traded snappy barbs with fellow writers Buddy and Sally. At home, he faced challenges with his wife Laura (played by Mary Tyler Moore) and son Ritchie. Van Dyke and Moore brought impeccable timing and a fluid choreography to their comedy. Many viewers tuned in to watch the attractive duo, who portrayed a positive image of a young, suburban couple during the early 1960s.

THE FUGITIVE

One of the decade's most revered shows was *The Fugitive*, starring David Janssen as Dr. Richard Kimble, a man wrongly convicted of killing his wife. On the way to death row, he is able to break free and spends four seasons (1963–1967) running from the law and trying to prove his innocence. In the finale, Kimble is finally cleared of the crime, which was actually committed by a one-armed man. That final episode was the most watched program to air on television at that time. The show also inspired a successful feature-length film, starring Harrison Ford, in 1993.

SPACE SERIES

Science fiction television programs actually began airing as early as 1949 with *Captain Video and His Video Rangers,* a children's program. *Captain Video* introduced children to the sci-fi genre and was followed in the 1950s by such fare as *Space Patrol, Tom Corbett—Space Cadet, The Adventures of Superman* (based on the DC comic), and *Science Fiction Theatre.* As the space program developed during the 1960s, so did interest in science fiction.

In the 1960s two sci-fi shows spent three years each on the prime-time schedule: Irwin Allen's *Lost in Space* and Gene Roddenberry's *Star Trek.* Because of its elaborate special effects, *Lost in Space* was one of the most expensive shows ever made when it appeared in 1965. In its early black-and-white broadcasts, it was an eerie, space-age adaptation of *The Swiss Family Robinson*—an 1812 novel about a family shipwrecked in the East Indies. In time the show morphed into more of a children's program, focusing especially on the Robot and his famous tag line, "Danger, Will Robinson!" Allen produced two other sci-fi shows in the 1960s: *The Time Tunnel* and *Voyage to the Bottom of the Sea*.

Though the *Star Trek* franchise now has an annual convention, and leagues of fans known as Trekkies or Trekkers, when it originally aired, it had a small audience. Reruns eventually inspired spinoff series and feature films, making *Star Trek* one of the best known and most influential series of the 1960s.

SCIENCE FICTION

STAR TREK

In retrospect, it is difficult to imagine that the sci-fi series *Star Trek* was not a hit when it originally aired from 1966 to 1969.

However, the voyages of the starship *Enterprise* did not reach a wide audience until reruns, when fans became enamored with Captain Kirk, Mr. Spock, and one of television's first multicultural casts—which included television's first interracial kiss! *Star Trek* soon became a phenomenon, spawning all kinds of merchandise and creating a strong and devoted cult following. Eventually, *Star Trek* would inspire twelve feature-length films and five additional television series (including *Star Trek: The Next Generation* and *Deep Space Nine*).

BATMAN!

In 1966, one of ABC's biggest hits was *Batman,* based on the DC comic book character. Unlike the black-and-white, dramatic *Adventures of Superman* in the 1950s, *Batman* was played farcically. By emphasizing the look and feel of a comic book—with pop-art colors and exaggerated dialog—*Batman* was a conscious satire of the superhero genre. In counterpoint to the droll delivery of its two main actors, Adam West as Batman and Burt Ward as Robin, the program showcased some well-known character actors playing villains, including Burgess Meredith as the Penguin and Frank Gorshin as the Riddler.

EVENING SOAP OPERAS

When *Peyton Place* premiered in 1964, few people expected a soap opera to find success in prime time. Yet *Peyton Place*—a half-hour evening drama based on a novel and movie of the same name—became so popular by its second year that ABC aired new episodes three times a week! The show made stars of Mia Farrow and Ryan O'Neal, who played teenagers during its early run.

Two medical shows also exhibited strong soapy tendencies in their plots and acting: *Ben Casey* and *Dr. Kildare*. Both shows featured handsome actors in their lead roles and offered the first prime-time example of what became known as "suds and sex"—a reference to the melodramatic and sometimes risqué plots of soap operas. Their blend of romance and medicine paved the way for such medical dramas as *St. Elsewhere*, *ER*, and *Grey's Anatomy*.

YOUTH MOVEMENT

As this generation entered its teens and early twenties, television began to cater to this growing demographic. Popular sitcoms about teenagers included *The Patty Duke Show*, in which Duke played cousins who were identical-looking, though far from identical in their hair, dress, and personalities: one was a rowdy American, the other proper and British. *Gidget*, a 1959 movie about a plucky California teenager who learns to surf, became a popular television show in 1965 starring eighteen-year-old Sally Field.

Music shows also catered to the growing teen market and the rise of rock and roll. The two most popular network variety programs for teens were *Shindig!* and *Hullaballoo*. Both featured live performances of the latest music acts, along with a cast of regular dancers doing all the latest dance crazes.

Even crime shows got into the youth movement when *The Mod Squad* premiered in 1968. The show featured three young leads, two men and a woman, who were social misfits. Promotional ads for the show described them as: "One white, one black and one blonde." All had minor criminal records, which gave them "street cred," but were rehabilitated by their crime-fighting endeavors. *The Mod Squad* was a blatant attempt to cash in on the ever-growing teen market. And it worked.

The Mod Squad was true to its name and its era. Featuring a young black man with an Afro, a hip, long-haired, short-skirted "chick," and a hippy-beaded white guy, it won over kids with its unconventional look, and adults with its crime-fighting endeavors.

VARIETY

Throughout the 1960s, variety programs reflected the changing cultural landscape. Ed Sullivan continued to showcase new and popular bands—including rock acts like the Beatles, the Rolling Stones, the Mamas and the Papas, and the Doors. Sullivan's sets for these acts became increasingly colorful—even psychedelic—as the decade progressed. In 1967 comedian Carol Burnett premiered her own variety series, *The Carol Burnett Show*, which would become one of the most successful and respected variety shows in television history.

Whereas established performers like Dean Martin and Andy Williams had long-running traditional shows, younger stars began to host their own shows. The Smothers Brothers were given their own variety hour in 1967. With topical

The Smothers Brothers' variety show, which ushered out the 1960s, was a far cry from *The Ed Sullivan Show*, which had ushered it in. Though also featuring special guests, the Smothers Brothers' show was a satirical take on society and politics.

humor and guests like politically active folk singer Joan Baez, *The Smothers Brothers Comedy Hour* reflected the clash between youth culture and the entertainment establishment. Tom and Dick Smothers repeatedly battled censors over the content of the show—including controversial skits and satirical comments about the Vietnam War. In 1968 CBS abruptly canceled the show for being too political.

LAUGH-IN

Rowan & Martin's Laugh-In premiered in 1968. The variety show offered an irreverent, fast-paced look at the events of the day, along with a lot of wordplay, music, and slapstick comedy. A regular cast of comedians delivered topical one-liners and off-the-wall sketches while go-go dancers in body paint gyrated suggestively in bikinis. The show became such a cultural phenomenon that even President Richard Nixon once appeared on *Laugh-In* and delivered the show's most famous catchphrase: "Sock it to me!"

ESPIONAGE

Following World War II, the cold war between the United States and the Soviet Union (now Russia) had many world citizens worried about the future of the planet. Spying became a big concern among world leaders—and espionage novels and films such as the *James Bond* series were already quite successful.

These fears also manifested themselves on television in such Bond-inspired fare as *The Man from U.N.C.L.E.* and *Mission Impossible*. The sitcom *Get Smart* provided a satirical take on cold war espionage. Even the animated *Rocky and Bullwinkle*

Show, as the two separate shows came to be known, offered a satirical look at international tensions.

ROCKY AND BULLWINKLE

Rocky and His Friends was an animated show about the friendship between a flying squirrel and a moose that ran from 1959 to 1961. After the second season, the show was renamed *The Bullwinkle Show*, and it continued until 1964. The two shows presented satires of westerns, fairy tales, and even cold war espionage between the United States and the Soviet Union. The humor was sharp and double-edged: children could enjoy the zaniness while their parents could appreciate the wit. The show is now considered a cult classic.

SPIES BREAKING BARRIERS

Two 1960s espionage dramas broke barriers of racism and sexism. Premiering in 1965, *I Spy* featured one of the first TV teams of white and black actors in lead roles: Robert Culp and African American comedian Bill Cosby. Although three Southern stations refused to air the show, Cosby won three consecutive Emmy Awards for his role.

Meanwhile, the highly stylized British import *The Avengers* featured one of the first lead spies who was a woman—Diana Rigg as agent Emma Peel, partner to Patrick Macnee's John Steed. With her lethal martial arts abilities and striking looks, Peel was a precursor of todays' strong female characters like Sydney Bristow in *Alias* and Ziva David in *NCIS*.

SESAME STREET

Children's programming reached a new level of achievement when *Sesame Street* premiered on PBS in 1969. *Sesame Street* combined children's entertainment with education and social messages. Set on a city street, the show mixed real actors with

The characters on *Sesame Street* made learning fun, and have continued to do so for more than forty years. The characters Jim Henson
(*right*) created have become famous worldwide.

the lovable puppets of creator Jim Henson: the Muppets.

For more than forty years, *Sesame Street* has set a high standard for educational television. More than 120 countries produce versions of the show—making it the most widely distributed American program in the world.

DECADE IN REVIEW

On July 21, 1969, the world watched as astronaut Neil Armstrong became the first human to walk on the moon. Viewers were riveted to their television sets, just as they had been for President Kennedy's funeral and the Beatles' first appearance on *Ed Sullivan*. Scenes of student sit-ins and civil rights riots also glued viewers to their screens and influenced cultural perceptions. All of these events illustrate the power of televised images to create a shared cultural experience.

The 1969 television schedule indicates that long-running, traditional shows continued to attract large audiences: *Bonanza*, *Hogan's Heroes*, *Bewitched*, *The Andy Williams Show*, *Walt Disney's Wonderful World of Color*, and *The Lawrence Welk Show*. Evening game shows brought a touch of the risqué to viewers in the form of *The Dating Game* and *The Newlywed Game*. However, sitcoms reveal that the standard TV fare still consisted mostly of traditional family programs, such as *The Courtship of Eddie's Father*, *Mayberry R.F.D.*, and *My Three Sons*.

Still, *The Smothers Brothers Comedy Hour* and *Laugh-In* indicated that television was becoming more daring and presenting nontraditional viewpoints and images. But these shows were the exception—not the rule.

Though television programming at the end of the 1960s may seem conservative now, all of that was about to change.

The shooting of four student protesters at Kent State University in 1970 was traumatic for much of the nation. The constant replay of the shooting on national television did nothing to extinguish the flames.

THREE

THE 1970s:

Changing Values— Changing Times

THE 1970S WAS A DECADE OF RAPIDLY changing culture. Women entered the workforce in greater numbers, people of color began to appear more frequently in positions of power and on television, and sexual issues became the subjects of movies and television shows. The civil rights movement of the 1960s paved the way for many of these changes.

Americans experienced many historical moments of the 1970s through their television screens: when the Ohio National Guard at Kent State University shot and killed four student protesters in 1970, when President Richard Nixon resigned in 1974, and when American hostages were taken in Iran in 1979, all of these events were broadcast on the news.

Many consider the decade an era of excess: people were experimenting in their personal lives and pushing the boundaries of social norms. Personal issues that were once considered socially unacceptable were openly discussed. The too-sweet sitcom *The Brady Bunch* may still have been going strong, but new sitcoms of the 1970s would challenge traditional views of the family. The innocent days of *Leave It to Beaver* in the 1950s were long gone.

Popular culture reflected societal changes in the 1970s as television began to address subjects it had never before acknowledged. While there were plenty of "fluff" programs on the air—from *Charlie's Angels* to *Love, American Style*—television reached new levels of sophistication in shows that are considered classics today, including *Mary Tyler Moore, Lou Grant,* and *M*A*S*H.*

TRADITIONAL BEGINNINGS

As the decade began, the long-running westerns *Gunsmoke* and *Bonanza* were still popular, and Carol Burnett's playful variety show continued to draw audiences. The top-rated show for 1970 was a mild drama about a small-town doctor: *Marcus Welby, M.D,* starring Robert Young (from *Father Knows Best*). Even Lucille Ball was still finding an audience with her third sitcom, *Here's Lucy.* But change was in the airwaves.

SITCOMS TAKE A STAND

Although drama may seem to be the most appropriate platform for dealing with topical issues, sitcoms were first to break from their traditional role. In the 1970s, sitcoms began to deal directly with provocative issues, such as racism, homosexuality, and menopause. For example, *Maude* was one of the first TV shows to address the issue of abortion, and the satirical *Soap* featured TV's first openly gay character. Meanwhile, *Good Times, All in the Family, The Jeffersons,* and *Sanford and Son* featured African Americans in various socioeconomic settings.

The provocative sitcom *Three's Company*—about a straight man pretending to be gay so his landlord will allow him to room with two women—reflected the loosening morals of the decade. Meanwhile, the multicultural cast of *Room 222* dealt seriously with the personal and social issues facing high school teachers, such as race relations and gender roles.

MARY TYLER MOORE

In 1970 a sitcom about a thirty-year-old single woman altered the face of television comedy. Originally, *The Mary Tyler Moore Show* was supposed to revolve around a divorced woman, but the network executives thought that the audience was not ready. Moore played Mary Richards, a television newsroom producer, as a successful, independent woman who took birth control pills and—in the show's seven-year run—never married. For the most part, the character remained happily single—a first for television sitcoms.

Mary Tyler Moore also introduced a new approach to sitcoms. The show found humor and pathos in character interaction

Originally portraying housewife Laura Petrie on *The Dick Van Dyke Show*, Mary Tyler Moore "graduated" to playing an independent career woman on *The Mary Tyler Moore Show*. The show broke new ground both as a reflection of the growth of feminism in the national culture and as a character-driven rather than plot-driven comedy.

(rather than inventing crazy situations), and allowed characters to grow and change slowly. Accomplished actors like Edward Asner and Cloris Leachman fleshed out the supporting cast. The show won numerous Emmy Awards—including three for Moore—and many of its characters (like Valerie Harper's popular Rhoda) went on to have their own spin-off shows.

ALL IN THE FAMILY

In January 1971, a mid-season replacement would go on to become the most successful, and most revolutionary, sitcom of the 1970s. *All in the Family*, starring Carroll O'Connor as the bigoted but complex blue-collar worker Archie Bunker, was based on the British sitcom *Till Death Us Do Part*.

When it premiered, *All in the Family* sent shockwaves through the viewing audience. CBS actually ran a disclaimer before the first episode. Bunker used racial and ethnic slurs, barked tyrannically at his sweet wife Edith (played by Jean Stapleton), and constantly argued political and social topics with his liberal son-in-law Michael (whom he called "Meathead").

In its blue-collar humor, and especially in its complex and flawed main character, *All in the Family* reflected a side of American culture with roots in *The Honeymooners*. It directly tackled issues of racism, women's rights, and politics in honest and insightful ways. *All in the Family* also spawned two more TV hits by creator Norman Lear: *Maude*, starring Bea Arthur as Edith's outspoken liberal cousin, and *The Jeffersons*, the first TV series to feature an upper-class black family.

M*A*S*H

Based on a movie of the same name set in the Korean War, the television show *M*A*S*H*—which premiered in 1972—functioned as a commentary on the ongoing Vietnam War. *M*A*S*H* was anything but a typical sitcom. It was not shot in

M*A*S*H, though set during the time of the Korean War, was really a commentary on the Vietnam War. Arguably, it did as much to influence popular opinion against the war as the massive protests held for years all over the United States.

front of a live studio audience, but filmed like a movie. It also blended comedy and drama and dealt frankly with the personal and political horrors of war. Winning fourteen Emmys during its eleven-year run, M*A*S*H was anchored by a stellar ensemble cast led by Alan Alda as the sarcastic, lecherous surgeon Hawkeye Pierce. More than 100 million viewers tuned in for the final episode, which aired in 1983—making it the most-watched broadcast in United States history, a record that was not topped until Super Bowl XLIV in 2010.

HAPPY DAYS AND MORE

Inspired by creator Garry Marshall's own childhood, *Happy Days* was set in the 1950s and revolved around the all-American Cunningham family, their son Ritchie (played by Ron Howard), and his pseudo-thug friend Fonzie, played by Henry Winkler. Fonzie became a "breakout character," having a great cultural effect and gaining wide recognition. Marshall was unable to sell the pilot of *Happy Days* until the 1973 film *American Graffiti*, also starring Ron Howard, renewed interest in the 1950s. Nostalgia for the 1950s became a cultural phenomenon.

In another of Marshall's creations, *Laverne & Shirley*, Penny Marshall and Cindy Williams recalled the slapstick humor of *I Love Lucy*. The shows *Taxi* and *Barney Miller* offered ensemble casts who played off one another, and comedian Bob Newhart provided a more sophisticated comedy in *The Bob Newhart Show*.

JUMP THE SHARK

Ever wonder where that saying came from? In a 1977 episode of *Happy Days*, Fonzie actually jumps over a shark while water-skiing. By the 1990s, this ridiculous plot development became a phrase used to describe the moment when a show starts to lose its value and direction.

FAMILY DRAMAS

As self-help books, daytime talk shows, and pop psychology began to take hold in the 1970s, a number of TV dramas dealt openly with serious family issues. *The Waltons*—based on a book by Earl Hamner Jr.—told the story of a family with seven children struggling to make ends meet in rural Virginia during the Great Depression. Led by Richard Thomas as John-Boy, the eldest son, the Emmy-winning show looked at such social issues as racism, war, illness, and politics.

Another rural family drama that found a wide audience was *Little House on the Prairie*, based on the books by Laura Ingalls Wilder set in the late 1800s. The family's pioneer spirit was embodied especially in the father, Charles Ingalls (played by Michael Landon). *Little House* also helped usher in the "family hour"—a block of programming between 8 p.m. and 9 p.m., established by the Federal Communications Commission in 1975. Officially, the family hour lasted only until 1977 when it was overturned in court, but the preference for family-oriented viewing before 9 p.m. remains a strong one.

More contemporary angst appeared in *Family*, a show about the middle-class Lawrence family who live in Pasadena, California. The series dealt maturely and thoughtfully with such issues as breast cancer, infidelity, adoption, and senility. *Eight Is Enough*, featuring Dick Van Patten as the father of eight children, began on a lighter note, but when the actress who played his wife died, her character was not recast on the show, and Van Patten's character became a widower.

In 1973 a PBS documentary about a family named Loud brought a more realistic perspective on family life in the United States. *An American Family* focused especially on the breakup of Patricia and Bill Loud's twenty-one year marriage and the coming out of their gay son, Lance. Lance became the first openly gay person on television, and the Louds—

the first reality-TV stars—even made the cover of *Newsweek* magazine because of that!

DALLAS

Dallas was a prime-time soap opera that began as a five-part miniseries in 1978 and then ran for thirteen successful seasons. The show centered on the wealthy, dysfunctional Ewings—and especially the power-hungry oil baron J. R. Ewing (played by Larry Hagman). The adulterous J. R. was unhappily married to alcoholic Sue Ellen and repeatedly butted heads with his more ethical younger brother Bobby.

In 2011, the *New York Times* reflected that the show "seemed to power the era's culture, celebrating personal wealth." After someone shot J. R. at the end of the 1980 season, 84 million people tuned in to see who did it—one of TV's largest audiences for any show. People even wore T-shirts asking: "Who shot J. R.?" In 2012, a revised version of the show aired, featuring some of the characters from the original series.

FROM COMEDY TO DRAMA

When *The Mary Tyler Moore Show* went off the air in 1977, CBS tried something daring and spun off a character from the sitcom, Mary's boss, into an hour-long drama series titled *Lou Grant*. In the new series, the hard-hitting editor (still played by Edward Asner) relocated from Minneapolis to Los Angeles and was surrounded by a new cast. He and his reporters faced such topical problems as the mistreatment of war veterans, nuclear proliferation, and conditions in nursing homes. *Lou Grant* won thirteen Emmy Awards and a Peabody Award (an award given annually for excellence in television and radio) during its five-year run.

CRIME PAYS

Since the early days of *Dragnet* and *The Untouchables*, crime dramas have drawn large television audiences. Raymond Burr—who had helped popularize television crime fiction in the 1950s with *Perry Mason*—played a wheelchair-bound police chief in *Ironside*, which began in 1967 but continued successfully into the 1970s.

Some of the most popular crime series of the 1970s included *Kojak*, *Columbo*, and *The Streets of San Francisco*. These shows all featured older, established actors in the lead roles: Telly Savalas, Peter Falk, and Karl Malden, respectively. Television has often provided a venue for former movie and theater actors who often appeal to older viewers. Some of these characters and their trademark lines—like *Kojak*'s "Who loves you, baby?"—became recognizable to world audiences.

Shows created for a specific time period can have lasting effects far beyond their initial success. *Mission Impossible*, which ended its TV run in 1973, eventually spawned four blockbuster films in the mid–1990s and 2000s, the most recent opening to big box office at Christmastime in 2011. *Hawaii Five-O*, which debuted in 1969 and ran for twelve years, was revived successfully on television with a new, young cast in 2010.

VARIETY

In 1970 comedian Flip Wilson became the first African American to have a successful variety series. The show ran for four years and was frequently one of the top five shows on television. Wilson appealed to audiences of all races. He created popular characters, such as Geraldine, whom he played in drag, and a number of his lines ("The devil made me do it!") became catchphrases with viewers across the country. At the close of the 1970–1971 TV season, Ed Sullivan ended his variety series, which had premiered in 1948!

Though African Americans had been increasingly represented on television variety shows and sitcoms since the late 1960s, few were as outrageously comedic as Flip Wilson, or crossed quite as many lines. One of his most popular characters was Geraldine, whom he played in drag at a time when drag queens were far from acceptable in the mainstream.

Pop music duo Sonny & Cher hosted a popular variety show at that time, as did country singer Glen Campbell, siblings Donny and Marie Osmond, and rock-and-roll star Tom Jones. By 1979, however, there were no longer any standard variety shows on the prime-time schedule, as the genre was slowly losing popularity with viewing audiences. Many of the 1950s and 1960s baby boomers likely felt that the variety format was dated. In the next decade, musical acts would find a new and more powerful way to reach younger audiences.

SATURDAY NIGHT LIVE

In 1975, a late-night comedy show changed the face of television when *Saturday Night Live* premiered on NBC. Featuring guest hosts, musical guests, and a cast of comic actors known as the Not Ready for Prime-Time Players, *SNL* offered sketches satirizing cultural issues—from politics to TV commercials. The show quickly found a huge following, especially among viewers in their teens and early twenties. *SNL* has often been audacious and irreverent, offering scathing satires of topical issues, celebrities, and human behavior. The cast's zany characters—from Roseanne Roseannadanna to Mary Katherine Gallagher to Dooneese—have become immediately recognizable cultural figures.

Still on the air as of 2013, the show has made stars of such performers as Steve Martin, Chevy Chase, Eddie Murphy, Julia Louis-Dreyfus, Adam Sandler, Tina Fey, Will Ferrell, Jimmy Fallon, Amy Poehler, and Kristen Wiig.

Saturday Night Live was revolutionary when it aired in 1975, due to its scathing political commentary, youthful cast, and group of irreverent writers. It has since become an institution, still on the air more than thirty-five years later.

DECADE IN REVIEW

In many ways, popular television in the 1970s was a study in extremes, reflecting the cultural changes that defined the decade. Although many shows tackled difficult social and political issues, family-oriented shows with positive themes continued to attract large audiences. Both *The Waltons* and *Little House on the Prairie* were still going strong in 1979.

In *The White Shadow*, a white former professional basketball player retires and takes a job coaching in a mostly black inner-city high school, whereas *Fantasy Island* and *The Love Boat* offered pure escapist fun. Meanwhile, the hugely popular comedy-drama *The Dukes of Hazzard* focused on good times and fast cars in the rural South, eventually inspiring a feature length film of the same name in 2005.

Sitcoms could be serious, like *M*A*S*H*, or goofy, like *Mork and Mindy* (which featured comedian Robin Williams as an uninhibited alien from outer space). The successful sitcom *One Day at a Time* presented TV comedy's first divorced mother, played by Bonnie Franklin. Meanwhile, *Three's Company* continued to go for laughs with its slapstick humor and risqué take on modern morality.

In 1973, CBS's Saturday night prime-time schedule was *All in the Family*, *M*A*S*H*, *The Mary Tyler Moore Show*, *The Bob Newhart Show*, and *The Carol Burnett Show*. Many still cite this line-up as one of TV's most sophisticated and impressive blocks of comedy.

FOUR

THE 1980s:
Expanding Horizons

PEOPLE OFTEN ASSOCIATE THE 1980S WITH materialism and a shift toward personal fulfillment rather than community values. It was a decade of splurge shopping, personal fitness gurus, and an increasing number of single-parent families. With Ronald Reagan as president, the national feeling was one of optimism. But there were also some hard economic times in the 1980s. Americans faced a number of serious challenges, including unemployment, a growing number of homeless, and the spread of HIV/AIDS.

In 1986, people watched their TV screens in horror as the space shuttle *Challenger* exploded just seventy-four seconds after liftoff—killing all seven astronauts, including schoolteacher Christa McAuliffe. Then in 1989, people all over the world cheered as they watched the Berlin Wall come down.

Viewers' relationship to their televisions also began to change in the 1980s as VCRs, video games, and camcorders allowed people to interact with and control their television sets in new and exciting ways. Videocassettes played on VCRs allowed people to record their favorite shows or events and then watch them at their convenience. And more people were

paying for the new cable television service, which offered more choices for viewers but posed a challenge to the old network programmers.

CABLE TELEVISION

Today, television viewers have become so accustomed to having a great variety of programs and stations to choose from that cable channels may seem as if they have always existed. Cable television first became prominent in the 1980s, thanks in great part to the Cable Act of 1984, which deregulated the cable industry and prompted growth. In the early 1980s, the popular music video station MTV helped establish the broad national appeal of cable television.

Whereas networks such as ABC, NBC, and CBS have local stations (known as affiliates) that air their programs, cable stations may be either national or regional channels. For example, AMC, TNT, USA, MTV, and ESPN air the same programs across the country. Local stations do not change times or interrupt cable programming as they sometimes do for network TV, as in the case of breaking news stories, certain sporting events, or presidential speeches.

Some cable channels appeal to—or are targeted at—a certain audience, like Lifetime for women viewers or Nickelodeon for children. Others are based on genre, like CNN or MSNBC for news, Syfy for science fiction fans, and CMT for fans of country music. Because cable stations have different regulations than network stations, they are able to offer content that may be more violent or sexual in nature. By 1989, about 60 percent of American households with television were receiving cable service, mostly as a way to increase their viewing choices.

The explosion of the space shuttle *Challenger* was captured live—in all its horror—on national TV.

CLASSIC SITCOMS

Many critics consider the 1980s to be the golden era of sit-coms. This assessment is due in great part to the success and longevity of many network shows, including *Cheers*, *The Cosby Show*, *The Golden Girls*, *Murphy Brown*, *Roseanne*, and *The Wonder Years*. Comedian Bob Newhart struck gold with a second sitcom, *Newhart*, about a couple running an inn in Vermont. Today, these shows are considered milestones in sitcom history. They not only drew a wide audience in the 1980s but, like some of their important predecessors, they also found success in reruns with subsequent generations.

WHERE EVERYBODY KNOWS YOUR NAME

When *Cheers* premiered in 1982, it ranked seventy-seventh out of seventy-seven shows that aired that week. No one could have guessed that a sharply written sitcom about the denizens of a bar in Boston would last eleven years. Initially, the show was built around the romantic tension between bar owner and former professional baseball player Sam Malone and neurotic, intellectual barmaid Diane Chambers. After five seasons, Shelley Long—who played Diane—left and was replaced by Kirstie Alley as bar manager Rebecca Howe.

Cheers also dealt with some topical issues, including Sam's alcoholism and his reaction to a former teammate coming out as gay at the bar. *Cheers* followed in the footsteps of sitcoms like *The Mary Tyler Moore Show*, having an ensemble cast and well-developed characters. It would go on to win an amazing twenty-eight Emmy Awards.

FAMILY SITCOMS

The Cosby Show, created by comedian Bill Cosby, changed the way viewers "saw" African American families. The sitcom revolved around the Huxtables, an upper-middle-class black family, with a father who was an obstetrician and a mother who was a lawyer, living in a brownstone in New York. Cosby found humor in everyday situations, and many of the plots were taken directly from his stand-up comedy routines. The show won Emmys, Golden Globes, and NAACP Image Awards. *TV Guide* once claimed that *The Cosby Show* "almost single-handedly revived the sitcom genre" in the 1980s.

In addition to *The Cosby Show*, other 1980s sitcoms focused on family situations. Reflecting the political climate of the 1980s, *Family Ties* featured progressive baby-boomer parents, Steven and Elyse Keaton, dealing with their conservative, materialistic son Alex (played by Michael J. Fox). This comedic setup reversed the one in *All in the Family*, in which the son-in-law was liberal.

Roseanne, starring comedian Roseanne Barr, was about a blue-collar family struggling to make ends meet in difficult economic times. With its raw working-class humor, *Roseanne* was reminiscent of earlier sitcoms like *The Honeymooners* and *All in the Family*. *Roseanne* reflected reality for many Americans in the 1980s who did not drive vans or wear designer clothes—prominent status symbols of the decade.

A new network station, Fox, delivered its first prime-time series in 1986. *Married . . . with Children* was a crude satire of family life. The show focused on the dysfunctional marriage of Al and Peggy Bundy and their resentful relationship with their children. Many critics found it tasteless and anti-family, and some politically driven journalists known as watchdogs even tried to organize a boycott of the program.

Nostalgia for simpler times found voice in another family sitcom, *The Wonder Years*, set in the 1960s. Revolving around young Kevin Arnold (played by Fred Savage), the thoughtful show expressed the yearnings many baby boomers were feeling for their youth. Unlike most sitcoms, *The Wonder Years* used no laugh track—previously recorded laughter used in many sitcoms to prompt viewers to laugh at certain moments. The show was a mix of comedy and drama, becoming a so-called dramedy. In 1989, it won a prestigious Peabody Award for excellence in television broadcasting.

GREATER REPRESENTATION

A number of shows in the 1980s featured predominantly African American casts, including the sitcoms *227*, *Amen*, and *A Different World*. The variety series *In Living Color* premiered as a mid-season replacement in the 1989–1990 television season. Created by Keenen Ivory Wayans, the show featured a multiracial cast (including the Wayans brothers, Jim Carrey, and Jennifer Lopez as a dancing "fly girl") that skewered cultural stereotypes. Influenced by the music video craze, *In Living Color* brought a fast-paced urban vibe to television variety.

WORKING WOMEN

A number of 1980s sitcoms featured working women as their main characters. Set in Atlanta, *Designing Women* focused on four Southern women running a design firm and juggling their professional and personal lives. Reflecting how economic necessity sometimes creates "new" families, *Kate and Allie* featured Susan Saint James and Jane Curtin, formerly of *SNL*, as two single moms who live together to save money and to help each other raise their children.

Television's most famous working woman in the late 1980s was *Murphy Brown*, played by Candice Bergen. In the popular series, news anchor Brown is a recovering alcoholic who has stayed at the Betty Ford Clinic, a facility named after former First Lady Betty Ford (an activist who spoke openly about her own addictions to alcohol and painkillers). The show dealt frankly with Murphy Brown's addiction and her battle

PURE GOLD

One of the decade's most successful sitcoms was *The Golden Girls*, a show about older women sharing a home in Miami, Florida. Four veteran actresses with impeccable comedic timing played the leads: Bea Arthur, Betty White, Rue McClanahan, and Estelle Getty. Despite its often bawdy humor, the show addressed such serious topics as Alzheimer's disease, chronic fatigue syndrome, and loneliness among the elderly. *The Golden Girls* ran for seven seasons, and all four actresses won Emmys for their roles.

The bawdy humor evident throughout *The Golden Girls* was unleashed even in its second episode, "Ladies of the Evening," played by Rue McClanahan (*left*), Betty White (*center*), and Bea Arthur.

with breast cancer (prompting an increase in women getting mammograms). In the early 1990s, *Murphy Brown* would make headlines when the title character had a baby out of wedlock and Vice President Dan Quayle criticized the show.

AN EARLY FROST

In 1985, the made-for-TV movie *An Early Frost* aired on NBC. The film starred Aidan Quinn as Michael Pierson, a successful gay lawyer who becomes infected with HIV. Along the way his family must come to grips with his illness and the social stigma attached to it. Though the network had difficulty finding sponsors for the film, *An Early Frost* won a number of awards, including a Golden Globe, an Emmy, and a Peabody. And it paved the way for future films to address the issue.

CRIME DRAMAS

A number of dramas in the 1980s took a gritty, realistic approach to their subject matter. *Hill Street Blues* was a mid-season replacement when it premiered in 1981—but the edgy cop show introduced a new approach to crime drama. It included ongoing story arcs, choppy hand-held camera work, and well-developed characters. Winning an unprecedented twenty-one Emmy Awards in its first year, *Hill Street Blues* set the tone for future crime drama series like *NYPD Blue* and *Law & Order*.

Honey West in the 1960s and *Police Woman* in the 1970s opened the door for female TV private eyes and police detectives—but having two women as leads in a crime drama was unheard of before *Cagney & Lacey*. *Cagney & Lacey* (1982–1988) starred Tyne Daly and Sharon Gless as two working-class police detectives, one married with children and one single.

Hill Street Blues had a new approach to crime drama and a realistic, edgy tone that set the scene for long-running successors such as ***Law & Order***.

ST. ELSEWHERE

Medical drama took an abrupt turn with *St. Elsewhere*, which premiered in 1982. This dark look at life at St. Eligius, an underfunded Boston hospital, featured a strong ensemble cast and dealt with a number of personal and social issues, including addiction, rape, AIDS, and abortion. With *St. Elsewhere*, television drama moved further into realism. The show also referenced other television programs, such as *The Fugitive* and *The Mary Tyler Moore Show*—an indication of the significant and enduring role television series have played in American culture.

STYLISH DRAMAS

Two of the decade's most stylish dramas were *Miami Vice* and *Moonlighting*. The slickly produced *Miami Vice* featured Don Johnson and Philip Michael Thomas as detectives James Crockett and Ricardo Tubbs, undercover cops who wore Versace clothes and drove a Ferrari. Its fast-paced production was straight out of MTV, and the stars' pastel-colored designer clothes had a strong effect on fashion trends in the mid–1980s. The romantic dramedy *Moonlighting* featured Cybill Shepherd and Bruce Willis as private eyes Maddie Hayes and David Addison.

One of the decade's most successful programs was *L.A. Law*, a slick legal drama with an ensemble cast and a large and loyal following. Featuring women and characters of color in lead roles as successful lawyers, *L.A. Law* helped break cultural expectations. Multiple storylines wove throughout each episode, keeping viewers tuning in each week. The show made stars of Jimmy Smits, Blair Underwood, and Harry Hamlin.

Dynasty brought a campy, soap-opera sensibility to prime time in 1981. Veteran TV star John Forsythe starred as Blake

Carrington, a Colorado oil baron. Outrageous plots could not stop the show from inspiring a line of linens, furs, perfume, and tuxedos. Other popular prime-time soaps reflecting the excess of the 1980s included *Knots Landing* and *Falcon Crest*.

YOUTH MOVEMENT

Some dramas appealed specifically to young viewers. One of the Fox network's first programs, *21 Jump Street*, featured a youthful cast (including Johnny Depp) playing undercover cops tackling difficult teen problems. *The Young Riders*, a western, focused on a group of youthful Pony Express runners in the Nebraska Territory in the mid–nineteenth century.

FANTASY AND SCIENCE FICTION

Fantasy and science fiction again became prominent in the 1980s with *Beauty and the Beast* and *Quantum Leap*. In *Beauty and the Beast*, an updated version of the 1946 French film, a New York City lawyer (played by Linda Hamilton) discovers another world beneath the streets of Manhattan, where she meets and falls in love with a poetic beast (played by Ron Perlman). In the sci-fi adventure *Quantum Leap*, Scott Bakula played Dr. Sam Beckett, a man who could assume the appearance of other people at different times in the past.

In 1987 Gene Roddenberry finally gave many *Star Trek* fans what they had longed for—a new series, *Star Trek: The Next Generation*. The show, featuring Shakespearian stage actor Patrick Stewart as Captain Jean-Luc Picard, lasted twice as long as the original series, not ending until 1994.

Though not as popular in the United States until the 2000s, the British series *Doctor Who*, about the adventures of an eccentric, time-traveling humanoid called The Doctor, began in 1963 and ran continuously until 1989, and was revamped by BBC in 2005.

FOR BOOMERS ONLY

As many baby boomers entered their thirties, it was inevitable that a television show would directly target this audience. *Thirtysomething* featured an ensemble cast of characters struggling with the angst of fading youth and growing responsibilities in suburban Philadelphia. Although frequently criticized for its self-absorbed characters, the show touched on real issues of family, career, infidelity, and loneliness.

THE SIMPSONS

In 1987 British comedian Tracey Ullman revived the variety series with her quirky humor and a bevy of outlandish and often poignant characters. For breaks and commercial lead-ins Ullman used snippets of an edgy cartoon about a dysfunctional family named the Simpsons. The animated spots became so popular that the Simpsons were spun off into their own half-hour show.

The Simpsons has remained on the air for more than twenty years. Created by Matt Groening, the show focuses on a "typical" American family: dimwitted father Homer, sweet and strong mother Marge, talented whiz-kid Lisa, über-brat Bart, and the baby, Maggie. No subject is taboo on *The Simpsons*. Over the past two decades, the show has offered a spot-on satire of American life—from crazy children's shows to public schools to immigration.

When President George H. W. Bush lamented that he wished American families were more like the Waltons and less like the Simpsons, Bart Simpson responded in an episode: "Hey, we are just like the Waltons. We're praying for an end to the depression, too."

The Simpsons followed in the footsteps of sitcoms critical of society such as *All in the Family*, but—perhaps because the show is animated and its lead characters are children—it seems to get away with far more irreverence.

DECADE IN REVIEW

Changes in social values—including greater openness about sex and gender roles—were expressed on television throughout the decade. Prime-time network shows also began to appeal directly to younger audiences and contained flashy graphics and music videos.

The 1989–1990 prime-time schedule reveals that a number of established shows were still popular at the end of the decade, including *Cheers, Dallas, The Golden Girls, Roseanne, The Cosby Show, L.A. Law*, and *Murphy Brown*. Veteran stage actress Angela Lansbury starred in a popular folksy mystery series called *Murder, She Wrote*, and *Baywatch* offered simplistic plots and beautiful people in bathing suits.

Popular television also became more creative in the late 1980s. The drama *China Beach* told the story of the Vietnam War from the perspective of women at a hospital and recreational facility. *It's Garry Shandling's Show*—telecast on Showtime—was one of cable TV's first sitcom successes. As George Burns did in the 1950s, Shandling talked directly to the audience in this quirky show.

With the growing popularity of cable television, networks faced increased competition. By 1989, 53 million American homes had cable television. Networks knew they would have to develop new and inventive ways to attract viewing audiences.

FIVE

THE 1990s:

Setting New Standards

A SHOW ABOUT NOTHING. SIX FRIENDS in a coffee shop. A neurotic psychiatrist in Seattle. "The truth is out there." Popular television in the 1990s produced some of the medium's most enduring shows. From *Seinfeld* to *Friends* to *Frasier* to *The X-Files*, the decade provided an impressive variety of quality programming. By offering provocative and topical storylines, shows like *Law & Order*, *NYPD Blue*, and *Will & Grace* altered the landscape of network television.

This newfound openness and reinvigorated approach reflected political and cultural changes in the decade. In 1992 the country elected Bill Clinton as the forty-second president of the United States. At forty-six, Clinton was the third youngest president to take office. Clinton represented the baby boomer population; the first generation raised on television and now entering middle age. Their attitudes toward foul language and nudity were much more open than that of previous generations. That openness was reflected on television.

In 1993 the first sexual child abuse case was brought against pop singer Michael Jackson. Later that year, Jackson released a statement about his discomfort over the humiliation of being

A nation watched in fascination as the police gave chase to O. J. Simpson's white SUV when his estranged wife was found murdered—and continued to watch as his trial for the murder, and eventual acquittal, were televised as well.

strip-searched. He eventually settled the allegations out of court. In 1995 viewers were riveted by the televised murder trial of former football star O. J. Simpson, accused of murdering his ex-wife and her friend. The case captured national attention. Simpson, an African American, was acquitted, but the case revealed strong racial divides in responses to the televised trial and to the acquittal.

PREMIUM SITCOMS

With *The Cosby Show*, *Roseanne*, *The Golden Girls*, *Cheers*, and *Murphy Brown* on the prime-time schedule, the sitcom was ripe for fresh ideas. Whereas many of these sitcoms employed the standard work and/or family structure, a new show decided to try something a little different. Most of its lead characters rarely worked, and none were family members. Instead, *Seinfeld* revolved around the wacky life of a stand-up comedian living in New York. The inventive show opened the door for new sitcoms featuring stand-up comedians Ellen DeGeneres, Ray Romano, Drew Carey, Tim Allen, and Brett Butler.

SEINFELD

When it premiered as a summer replacement show in 1989, many viewers and critics considered *Seinfeld* too quirky to become a success. Set in New York, the show also seemed too "East Coast"—too urban in its characters and approach—for mass appeal. Yet, *Seinfeld* spoke to young professionals whose lives did not involve children and in-laws. Like George Burns and Jack Benny before him, Seinfeld played a fictional version of himself, and early episodes were framed by brief samples of his stand-up routine.

Seinfeld's "family" consisted of his three closest friends: chronically out-of-work George (Jason Alexander), sarcastic ex-girlfriend Elaine (Julia Louis-Dreyfus), and eccentric neighbor Kramer (Michael Richards). Focusing on all four characters' self-absorption and inability to find happiness, the show ushered in a darker kind of sitcom humor. During its nine seasons, it also introduced many minor characters that became household names, including the Soup Nazi, Jerry's irascible neighbor Newman, and George's over-the-top parents. In 2002, *TV Guide* named *Seinfeld* the greatest television program of all time.

FRASIER

Kelsey Grammer played psychiatrist Frasier Crane for years on *Cheers* before his character was spun off into his own show in 1993. Set in Seattle, *Frasier* focused on the title character's own neuroses in his dealings with family members and coworkers. With its razor-sharp writing and well-developed characters, *Frasier* became one of television's most-respected sitcoms—proving that the medium could be so much more than a place for couch potatoes. The show won an unprecedented thirty-seven Emmys during its eleven-year run.

FRIENDS

The simply named *Friends* took the concept of sitcoms about groups of singles to another level. One of the most successful shows in television history, the sitcom featured six friends in their twenties—three men and three women—living in New York. The characters were attractive and endearing, and the show avoided topics that were dark or disturbing.

Crisply written, often in short scenes moving at a rapid pace, *Friends* quickly found its audience. The show's appeal was evident when Jennifer Aniston's hair-do (called "the Rachel" after her character), a heavily layered, lightly highlighted, shoulder-length style, became a national phenomenon that remained popular throughout the decade. Meanwhile, her character's on-again, off-again romance with David Schwimmer's Ross frequently held the audience captivated, indicating how involved viewers can become with fictional characters on television. The formula of this show's cast has been imitated again and again, most successfully by *How I Met Your Mother*.

CATCHPHRASES

How much does TV influence language? Consider phrases "yadda, yadda, yadda" and "master of your domain" from *Seinfeld*. Fans of *Friends* frequently imitated Joey's pick-up line, "How *you* doin'?" or Chandler's rhetorical "Could I *be* any more—?" All of the *Friends* characters' use of the word "so"—as in "that is *so* not going to happen"—also became a national trend. Television has a long history of generating catchphrases—from The Robot's "Danger, Will Robinson" on *Lost in Space* to the waitress Flo's "Kiss my grits" on *Alice* to "GTL" (gym, tanning, laundry) from *The Jersey Shore*.

ELLEN COMES OUT

In 1994, comedian Ellen DeGeneres hit the airwaves with her sitcom *These Friends of Mine*, loosely based on the *Seinfeld* format. After the first season the show's name changed to *Ellen*—but a greater change occurred in 1997 when DeGeneres announced to the world that she was gay. Conservative groups began to boycott the show, and ABC started to run a parental advisory about content at the beginning of each episode. Although it was cancelled in 1998, *Ellen* paved the way for other openly gay characters.

WILL & GRACE

A sitcom about a gay man living with a straight woman would have been unheard of in the 1970s, but when *Will & Grace* premiered in 1998 audiences happily embraced it. Cultural attitudes toward homosexuality had shifted in the four years since Ellen premiered, and television was aiding in that shift. Plots revolved around Will Truman, a gay lawyer, and his long friendship with Grace Adler, an interior designer; the two lived together in an apartment in New York.

While both Eric McCormack and Debra Messing brought a certain amount of reality to the two title characters, Megan Mullally and Sean Hayes played cohorts Karen and Jack in broad slapstick gestures. Boozy Karen "worked" for Grace in her design firm, and Jack was a would-be actor and dancer often living off his friend Will.

EVERYBODY LOVES RAYMOND

One of TV's most popular sitcoms in the 1990s was *Everybody Loves Raymond*, starring stand-up comedian Ray Romano. The show found its comic tension in the relationship between sportswriter Ray Barone and his sardonic wife Debra (played by Patricia Heaton). But two veteran character actors—Peter Boyle and Doris Roberts—often stole the show as Ray's neurotic parents Frank and Marie. Although the setup seemed traditional, the familial tensions were sometimes dark and played seriously. Many cast members won Emmy Awards for their work on the show, including Brad Garrett, who won three Emmys for his role as Ray's put-upon older brother Robert.

DARK DRAMAS

The 1990s were undoubtedly the decade of crime drama— thanks in great part to the success of *Law & Order* and *NYPD Blue*. The plotlines of these shows were often "ripped from the headlines," or taken from actual news events. Their approach was darker and more realistic than TV dramas from previous decades. Some strong adult language—which had never before been allowed on network television—also began to creep into these productions.

Law & Order premiered in 1990 and has seemingly never stopped. Though the original show went off the air in 2010, *Law & Order: SVU* remains on the air, as does *Law & Order: UK*, and a constant loop of reruns. The series' ripped-from-the-headlines appeal has far outlasted the current events on which the episodes are based.

Law & Order premiered in 1990 and ran for an impressive twenty years. Its cast changed periodically, but its format remained the same. In the first part of the show, after a crime scene was shown, detectives searched for clues to find the perpetrator(s). The second part focused on the prosecuting lawyers as they worked to convict the accused. Viewers got two shows for the price of one: a police procedural and a courtroom drama.

Filmed in New York City, *Law & Order* exuded a gritty realism while utilizing the talents of great character actors who lived in New York. Such powerful stage actors as Sam Waterston, Jerry Orbach, and S. Epatha Merkerson brought special life to their recurring characters over the years.

The much-admired show won Emmy Awards, Golden Globes, NAACP Awards, and Edgar Awards (given for works in the mystery genre). It also inspired successful spin-offs, such as *Law & Order SVU* (focusing on sexually based crimes) and *Law & Order: Criminal Intent* (which altered the format by often revealing the perpetrator early on in the episode). *Law & Order UK* began being televised in the United Kingdom in 2009 and can be seen on cable network BBC America in the United States, as well.

NYPD BLUE

NYPD Blue premiered in 1993 on ABC and shook censors with its frequent profanity and partial nudity. Unlike *Law & Order*, *NYPD Blue* focused on the personal lives of its characters, especially that of Detective Andy Sipowicz (played by Dennis Franz). The edgy police procedural was one of the first shows to predominantly feature hand-held camera work, giving scenes a sometimes choppy, realistic feel. With shows like *NYPD Blue*, the limits of material considered acceptable for network television were being challenged.

ER

Medical dramas reached a new pinnacle when *ER* hit the airwaves in 1994. Author Michael Crichton and film director Steven Spielberg originally produced the show featuring an ensemble cast that included George Clooney, Anthony Edwards, Julianna Margulies, Eriq La Salle, and Noah Wyle. The longest-running prime-time medical drama to air on American television, *ER* received 124 Emmy nominations during its fifteen-year run—the most so far of any television show!

QUIRKY DRAMAS

Two dramas revolved around the challenges of small-town life in the 1990s: *Northern Exposure* and *Twin Peaks*. *Northern Exposure* (1990–1995) was set in the fictional town of Cicely, Alaska, and focused on the life of a Jewish doctor from New York trying to adapt to the oddities of the Alaskan town and its people. *Twin Peaks*, set in a small fictional town in Washington State, was created by experimental film director David Lynch and writer Mark Frost. The psychological thriller followed the search for the murderer of Laura Palmer.

Though the series had a cult following, it ran on ABC for only thirty episodes in 1990–1991 before it was canceled. Many questions regarding the death of Laura Palmer were left unanswered. However, fans of the show received closure in 1992 when the film *Twin Peaks: Fire Walk with Me* was released and resolved all of the show's storylines.

ALLY MCBEAL

Drama and comedy blended seamlessly in the legal series *Ally McBeal*, which premiered on Fox in 1997. The show focused on the personal and professional escapades of the title character, a lawyer played by Calista Flockhart. The often stressed-out McBeal sometimes hallucinated visions, including a dancing baby. The show also addressed issues about the role of women in the workplace. In 1998 a *Time* magazine cover depicted the fictional McBeal with real-life feminists Gloria Steinem, Betty Friedan, and Susan B. Anthony and asked: "Is feminism dead?" The article's author took issue with the commercialism driving the success of characters like McBeal and called them "pseudo-feminists." The article and the show provoked an ongoing discussion in the media about what determines a feminist.

SCI-FI AND FANTASY

Science fiction and fantasy fans found a bonanza of TV programs in the 1990s—thanks in great part to fledgling cable networks like Fox, the WB, and UPN. Fox led the pack with the eerie and hugely popular *The X-Files*. Meanwhile, *Star Trek* fans were treated to new adventures in *Star Trek: Voyager*—the first series shown on UPN.

In 1997, the WB struck gold with *Buffy the Vampire Slayer*, a teen coming-of-age drama starring Sarah Michelle Gellar as Buffy Summers, a teenager who begrudgingly accepts that the universe "chose" her to be the next vampire slayer. The show helped to usher in the popular teen-vampire genre and also instituted a more complex style of teen drama.

Some fantasy shows were syndicated—meaning they could be sold to and shown on various stations around the country. Two popular syndicated fantasy series in the 1990s were *Hercules: The Legendary Journeys* and its spin-off *Xena: Warrior Princess*, both of which were cult favorites.

Based on a movie from which it quickly strayed, *Buffy the Vampire Slayer* became a runaway hit with teenagers, and can be said to have ushered in the "good" vampire era that has lasted to this day.

THE X-FILES

Detective story met science fiction in Fox's haunting series *The X-Files*. The dark program featured David Duchovny and Gillian Anderson as Fox Mulder and Dana Scully, two FBI agents looking for the truth behind paranormal events, UFOs, and aliens. Whereas Mulder was a believer in all things paranormal, Scully remained skeptical, creating the show's central conflict. The show's opening tag line was "The Truth is out there," and it played to conspiracy theories and government cover-ups. *The X-Files* became so popular during its nine-year run (1993–2002) that it spawned two feature-length films, one in 1998 and the other in 2008. The show was also one of the first to be frequently discussed by fans online.

YOUTHFUL ENDEAVORS

A number of successful shows appealed directly to younger audiences. Fox's immensely popular *Beverly Hills, 90210*, premiering in 1990, led the way with its young attractive cast playing high school students from the exclusive zip code. It made teen idols out of stars Luke Perry and Jason Priestly—and had an equally successful spin-off, *Melrose Place*.

The WB's *Felicity* (1998–2002) starred Keri Russell as a first-year college student facing the challenges of living in New York City. Other popular teen-oriented shows in the 1990s included the racy *Dawson's Creek*, about four friends in a fictional Massachusetts town, and the more conservative *7th Heaven*, about a Protestant minister's family living in a fictional California town. All of these shows dealt with a number of serious issues, including teenage suicide, date rape, racism, and homelessness.

The critically acclaimed *My So-Called Life* featured Claire Danes as angst-ridden fifteen-year-old Angela Chase, and dealt openly with such social issues as homophobia, school violence, and teenage alcoholism. *Party of Five*, a show about five orphans who must take over running their parents' restaurant, premiered in 1994 and was nearly canceled after its first year—until it won a Golden Globe Award.

THE WEST WING

Political issues took center stage in the presidential drama *The West Wing*, starring Martin Sheen. Premiering in 1999 at the end of Bill Clinton's presidency, *The West Wing* starred Martin Sheen as U.S. President Josiah Bartlet, a liberal Democrat with some military leanings. The show focused on professional and personal intrigue in the White House and spoke especially to liberal viewers who thought that President Clinton, a Democrat, had been too moderate in many of his decisions. *The West Wing* won twenty-seven Emmy Awards.

GAME SHOWS ASCENDING

Game shows have a long history dating back to the 1950s with *Twenty-One* and *The $64,000 Question*. When it came out that many of these shows were rigged, producers faced a Congressional hearing. Other early prime-time game shows included *What's My Line?* and *I've Got a Secret*.

Game shows began to be featured more on daytime television during the mid–1960s. *Let's Make a Deal* began in 1963, and *Jeopardy!* premiered in 1964. Both *The Price Is Right* and *Wheel of Fortune* began in the 1970s. All of these games shows were still on the air as of 2013.

In 1999 an American version of a British program became one of the most successful prime-time game shows in TV history. *Who Wants to Be a Millionaire* aired on the ABC network and became syndicated in 2002. Originally hosted by Regis Philbin, *Millionaire* became a huge hit. Network executives

The success of the 1999 prime-time game show *Who Wants to Be a Millionaire* proved to be the precursor of a whole decade of reality TV programs.

realized that there was an audience for game shows and reality television programs, which are much less expensive than a comedy or drama series. The success of *Millionaire* and the desire to produce more cost-effective programming would lead to the boom in reality TV in the following decade.

DECADE IN REVIEW

Prime-time television in the 1990s reflected greater openness about politics, language, and sexuality—especially teenage sexuality—in American culture. Many programs also played more directly to youthful audiences, indicating a shift in viewership away from an older, more conservative audience. Real people and real events began to influence prime time also, first as headlines influencing storylines on crime shows but eventually as its own genre, reality TV.

The Daily Show with Jon Stewart, a satirical news program beginning in 1996, blended humorous commentary of the news with real interviews with public figures. In the next decade *The Daily Show* would spawn an equally humorous political spin-off, *The Colbert Report*, featuring former *Daily Show* correspondent Stephen Colbert.

In 1998, comedian Drew Carey, in addition to his own sitcom, began to host a half-hour improv show, *Whose Line Is It Anyway?* Just as *Happy Days* had played to nostalgia for the 1950s in the 1970s, the sitcom *That 70s Show* looked at teenage years in the 1970s. Accomplished stage and film actor John Lithgow starred in the farcical *3rd Rock from the Sun*, about aliens adapting to life on Earth.

Thanks to the success of *The Simpsons*, more animated sitcoms appeared on the schedule, including *King of the Hill*, *South Park*, *Family Guy*, and *Futurama*. These shows were also extremely satirical in their view of American life and culture.

Prime-time news programs were also quite popular in the 1990s: ABC offered *20/20*, NBC had *Dateline NBC*, and CBS lead the pack with its long-running and much admired *60 Minutes* (which first aired in 1968). Following in the footsteps of Barbara Walters, more women became national news anchors in the 1990s, including Katie Couric (the first woman to anchor an evening news show solo) and Diane Sawyer. More black and Hispanic newscasters also appeared on television throughout the decade.

Most interesting is the continued appearance of the reality programs *COPS* and *The Real World*. On *COPS*, which premiered on FOX in 1989, cameras followed law enforcement officials during patrols and various police activities. Meanwhile, *The Real World*—which premiered on MTV in 1992—featured a group of young strangers living together under video surveillance. These two reality shows were only the tip of a cultural iceberg that was about to surface in full force in the next decade of popular television.

SIX

THE 2000s:

Reality and Reality TV in the First Decade

TELEVISION VIEWERS ALL OVER THE WORLD were glued to their TV screens on September 11, 2001, during the attacks on the World Trade Center in New York and the Pentagon in Washington, D.C. Footage of the planes crashing into the towers—and of the towers falling—was seared into the public consciousness. More than ever before, television transcended geographic and cultural boundaries to unite the world in horror and grief.

As the decade progressed, the rise of computer and cell phone usage among young people began to replace television viewing with personal alternatives that no one in the decades before could have guessed would ever become a reality. During the 1990s, cable television stations had produced more first-run series vying for viewers' attention. Perhaps the greatest threat

By the turn of the century, television screens were everywhere, in-cluding this enormous one in New York City's Times Square, where people watched the destruction of the World Trade Center towers on September 11, 2001. By the end of the decade, screens were both tiny and large, with millions watching programs on their smartphones.

to popular network programming came from the widespread growth of the Internet. The Internet, which expanded by leaps and bounds in the 1990s, and the acquisition of personal computers, offered people a new and even more convenient source of entertainment. As an alternative to television people could visit websites and view content whenever they wanted—they were not restricted to television's schedule.

In 2006 ABC became the first network to stream shows online. People could more easily download or stream videos, programs, and full-length movies to watch at their convenience. These choices posed a challenge to both network and cable channels. Television needed to step up its game to compete with these new alternatives to TV viewing—especially among the young.

REALITY TV

The American pop artist Andy Warhol once observed: "In the future, everyone will be world-famous for fifteen minutes." If he could have foreseen the phenomenon known as reality television, he might have revised that prediction beyond a mere fifteen minutes. Reality TV spoke to the idea that anyone could be a star—and that even the worst behavior could be worthy of televised attention.

Although many people associate reality TV with the past ten years, television has featured unscripted "reality" programming since the late 1940s. The show *Candid Camera*, for example, featured people set up by actors in awkward situations. Hidden cameras then filmed their often-humorous reactions. The show became so popular that it ran, off and on, on different channels from 1948 to 2004.

Economics played a large role in the growth of reality programs in the 2000s. Production costs for a reality program are much lower than those for scripted dramas and comedies.

Reality programs are less of a financial risk for networks, especially during a time when television viewership is dwindling.

In addition to the growth of reality programming, cable channels also began to produce more successful series vying for the attention of network TV viewers in the first decade of the 2000s. Some of these shows, like *The Sopranos*, *Sex and the City*, and *Mad Men*, would become cultural milestones.

REAL BEGINNINGS

Two reality programs that premiered in 2000 became hugely popular with viewers: *Big Brother* and *Survivor*. *Big Brother* features contestants who are living together under constant surveillance and are eliminated one by one. The final contestant wins a large cash prize. *Big Brother* has been a prime-time hit in more than seventy countries.

A summer replacement program premiering in 2000, *Survivor* was the first mega-hit in the reality TV universe. Isolated in the wilderness, contestants must complete tasks to survive life in the wild but must also avoid being voted off by the other contestants. More than 50 million viewers watched the first season's finale.

AMERICAN IDOL

In June 2002, a reality singing contest based on a British show called *Pop Idol* took the United States and, in time, most of the rest of the world by storm. *American Idol* features amateur singers competing for viewers' votes to avoid elimination—the last one standing wins a recording contract. The show originally had an innocent quality, full of young, ambitious performers and some people with poor estimations of their singing ability, resulting in humorously bad auditions. As each year has passed, however, the show has become increasingly sophisticated in production values.

American Idol, **launched in 2002, was a reality singing contest tapping deeply into one aspect of the American dream: the idea that anyone could become a star, given the right opportunity.**

As in the British version, *American Idol* also employs three knowledgeable judges who critique the contestants' performances: originally these were creator Simon Cowell, singer and dancer Paula Abdul, and musician Randy Jackson. When Cowell and Abdul left *American Idol*, rock musician Steven Tyler and singer and dancer Jennifer Lopez were added to the judges' table. The following season saw R&B singer Mariah Carey, hip-hop artist Nicki Minaj, and country star Keith Urban introduced as judges. This format has proven to be a template for reality competitions involving performance.

IDOL'S A WINNER!

From 2002 to 2013, *American Idol* topped the ratings charts eight times—the first show ever to have done so in the history of television. Since season seven, the songs contestants sing on each episode have been made immediately available for purchase on iTunes, indicating the increasing importance of Internet access to television success. As of 2013, *American Idol* is broadcast to more than one hundred countries worldwide—and many have their own versions, as well.

PERFORMANCE SHOWS

The enormous success of *American Idol* prompted the creation of other televised contests. One of the most popular is *Dancing with the Stars*, which premiered in 2005 (based on another British series, *Strictly Come Dancing*). In this show celebrity contestants—from actors to models to politicians to sports figures—dance with professional dancers until all but one pair is eliminated.

Another dance contest, *So You Think You Can Dance*, pits young, amateur dancers against each other in choreographed competitions and weekly eliminations. With its youthful contestants, the show has brought an appreciation for dance to a large young audience since 2005. Both *Dancing with the Stars* and *So You Think You Can Dance* employ a panel of judges.

Fox's *America's Got Talent* by contrast has a circus-like quality about it. Contestants can be performers of any format—from jugglers to singers to magicians—and of any age.

THE APPRENTICE

In 2004, billionaire businessman Donald Trump created a competition for aspiring entrepreneurs: *The Apprentice*.

Contestants compete to win a coveted place running one of Trump's many businesses. In its seventh season, *The Apprentice* began to use celebrity contestants who competed for charities. It returned briefly to its original format in 2010, but continued with celebrity contestants in later seasons. Trump's catch phrase "You're fired!" has been imitated by many fans of the show.

CABLE HITS

Two programs on premium cable channel HBO became cultural benchmarks in the early twenty-first century: *Sex and the City* and *The Sopranos*. Both began in the late 1990s, but their popularity exploded the following decade.

Sex and the City, based on a book of the same name by Candace Bushnell, premiered in the summer of 1998. The often risqué show revolved around four women in their thirties: narrator and sex columnist Carrie Bradshaw (played by Sarah Jessica Parker), no-nonsense attorney Miranda Hobbes (Cynthia Nixon), art dealer-turned-housewife Charlotte York (Kristin Davis), and vampy PR agent Samantha Jones (Kim Cattrall). Stylish, daring, and topical, the show captured viewers' attention with its overtly female perspective and strong character development. The show became so popular that it brought about NYC tours of the real bars, shops, and neighborhoods the four fictional friends frequented. It also spawned two feature-length films in 2008 and 2010.

The Sopranos premiered in 1999 and is considered one of television's most innovative dramas. Although focusing on the personal life of Mafia leader Tony Soprano (played by James Gandolfini), the show presented a deep character study and thoughtful, intelligent scripts. Many critics consider it as one of television's best shows. During its eight-year run, *The Sopranos* won twenty-one Emmys and five Golden Globes for its powerful acting and strong cinematic style.

The hit HBO show *Sex and the City* was just one of the series that brought the cable network into prominence. It also changed the way women worldwide viewed themselves, giving a risqué twist to the idea of sexual and feminist liberation.

OTHER CABLE HITS

Another important cable offering was Showtime's *Weeds*, a darkly comic show that premiered in 2005 and ended in 2012. *Weeds* revolved around the life of Nancy Botwin, a suburban mother of two played by Mary-Louise Parker, who sells marijuana to make ends meet after her husband dies. The edgy show won two Emmys, a Golden Globe, and a Writers Guild of America Award.

Meanwhile, HBO's *Big Love* (2006–2011) focused on Bill Henrickson (played by Bill Paxton), a polygamist Mormon in Utah who is married to three women. The show addressed the personal and political battles Henrickson's family members faced because of their alternative lifestyle.

MAD MEN

Set in a 1960s advertising agency, *Mad Men* tells the story of Don Draper, an ad man who has taken another man's identity. Played with impeccable style by Jon Hamm, Draper is surrounded by well-drawn characters, including aspiring copywriter Peggy Olson, caught-between-two-eras Joan, and hard-drinking agency partner Roger Sterling.

Mad Men offers an insightful depiction of a significant era in American history, when advertising—especially television advertising—was becoming a driving force in the country's consumer culture. Women were questioning their traditional roles as housewives and entering the workplace in greater numbers. Racism, sexism, and homophobia were still problems—but as the well-written show reveals, boundaries were beginning to be pushed. *Mad Men* addresses all of these issues on a very personal, human level.

The AMC cable show *Mad Men* brought to life the way society was in the early 1960s—racist, sexist, classist, as well as on the verge of deep change. It also gave rise to a number of retro clothing lines and cocktails.

A period piece offering deep commentary on American consumer culture, *Mad Men* is the first cable series (on AMC) to win the Emmy Award for Outstanding Drama Series four years in a row (2008–2011).

CRIME PAYS

Crime procedural programs remained popular throughout the 2000s, and the three most watched shows were *CSI*, *NCIS*, and *Bones*. When it premiered in 2000, *CSI: Crime Scene Investigation*—focusing on a forensic team in the Las Vegas police department—helped inspire interest in forensics-driven programs. *CSI* became so popular that it created a franchise, resulting in two more shows: *CSI: Miami* and *CSI: New York*.

NCIS's popularity stemmed from its engaging ensemble cast, featuring Mark Harmon as Special Agent Leroy Jethro Gibbs and his cohorts Anthony DiNozzo, Ziva David, Timothy McGee, and Abby Sciuto. Tight writing and strong chemistry among the actors have made *NCIS* a consistent ratings winner since 2003.

A different kind of chemistry sizzles on *Bones*, a show focused on forensic anthropology and archeology in cases involving the FBI. Emily Deschanel plays brainy anthropologist Dr. Temperance "Bones" Brennan, and David Boreanaz plays her brawny partner, Special Agent Seeley Booth. Sexual chemistry between the two leads drives much of the popular show's tension.

Audiences enjoy these shows because forensic science solves crimes with a degree of certainty, giving the fictional plots a sense of closure that appeals to the viewer.

WOMEN ON THE BEAT

Other popular crime dramas include *Medium* (2005–2011), with Patricia Arquette as a psychic working with a district attorney in Phoenix, and *The Closer* (2005–2012), starring

Kyra Sedgwick as a Southern police chief who has been transferred to Los Angeles where she faces sexism on the job. Both Arquette and Sedgwick won Emmy Awards for their powerful, layered portrayals of their lead characters.

HOSPITAL DRAMAS

Following in the footsteps of *St. Elsewhere* and *ER*, *Grey's Anatomy* and *House M.D.* have won fans with their blend of personal drama and medical procedure. Narrated by its main character, intern Meredith Grey (played by Ellen Pompeo), *Grey's Anatomy* focuses on the struggles of a multi-racial group of interns and doctors at Seattle Grace Mercy West Hospital. *House M.D.* centers on Dr. Gregory House, a tyrannical medical genius played by Hugh Laurie, who, with his team of doctors, must diagnose strange symptoms and treat often-rare diseases. Laurie drives the show with his powerful portrayal of the brilliant but flawed doctor.

FRIDAY NIGHT LIGHTS

Based on the film of the same name, the highly acclaimed drama series *Friday Night Lights*—about a high school football team in fictional Dillon, Texas—ended its four-year run in 2011. Originally airing on NBC, it was later picked up by Direct TV when NBC pulled the series from its fall line-up and slated it to air during the summer. Using football as a metaphor for American life, *Friday Night Lights* was a prime example of a television series commenting on and reflecting cultural challenges.

SUCCESSFUL "DRAMEDIES"

A number of hour-long programs have struck gold by cleverly combining elements of drama and comedy in ongoing story arcs. Three of the decade's most popular dramedies were *Ugly Betty*, *Desperate Housewives*, and *Glee*. *Ugly Betty* (2006–2010) starred America Ferrera as Mexican American Betty Suarez, a fashion-challenged young woman aspiring to be part of the fashion publishing world. Each episode featuring her trials at work was a little morality tale that won viewers' affection for an underdog who ultimately triumphed.

Desperate Housewives (2007–2012) offers a sometimes-farcical yet often poignant satire of American suburban life. Focusing on the lives of four attractive neighbors on fictional Wisteria Lane, *Desperate Housewives* mixed soap opera melodrama with sitcom comedy.

A show about a high school singing group, *Glee* premiered in 2010 and became an instant hit with its angst-ridden teen plotlines and show-stopping musical numbers. The show speaks especially to teens who feel as if they are different. It deals openly with issues such as bullying, teen pregnancy, homophobia, and peer pressure. Its flashy production often reflects the influence of music videos on the performing arts. *Glee* has also inspired increased interest in show choirs and glee clubs in high schools around the world.

RETURN OF THE SITCOM

As the decade progressed, the half-hour sitcoms *Frasier*, *Will & Grace*, and *Friends* came to an end—and many critics felt that the sitcom format was near extinction. That prediction turned out to be premature.

CBS's *Two and a Half Men* premiered in 2003. The hugely popular show featured Charlie Sheen as successful jingle-writer and lady's man Charlie Harper and Jon Cryer as his divorced, sad-sack brother Alan. It would become one of the most successful sitcoms of the decade, primarily based on the outrageous dialog. Sheen's public battle with Chuck Lorre, the show's creator—and his demands for more money—resulted in his being fired from the series in 2011 and replaced by Ashton Kutcher, who had starred in *That 70s Show* in the 1990s.

The standard sitcom format changed somewhat with a number of new shows. Starring Jason Bateman, the wry sitcom *Arrested Development* perfected the one-camera method (the show was not filmed in front of an audience) in this show about a wacky, dysfunctional family.

In a similar style, the quirky sitcom *The Office*—based on a British series of the same name—starred Steve Carell (until 2011) as the regional manager of a fictional paper company in Scranton, Pennsylvania. Airing from 2005-2013, the offbeat show was inventive in its use of the characters' personal confessions, which were delivered directly to the camera.

30 Rock was created by Tina Fey, a former writer for, and star of, *Saturday Night Live*. Fey took many of her experiences as head writer for *SNL* and turned them into scripts for the award-winning sitcom. The show's title is a reference to 30 Rockefeller Plaza, the address where *SNL* is filmed and where NBC's New York office is located. Fey has won both writing and acting awards for her work on *30 Rock*.

How I Met Your Mother is told in flashbacks as a father recalls memories of his years as a single man living in New York City. The strong ensemble—with Neil Patrick Harris stealing the show with his brash portrayal of womanizer Barney Stinson—clicked immediately with viewers. Its innovative format keeps viewers guessing about the identity of the title's "mother."

Modern Family, premiering in 2009, reflects changing social norms about what constitutes a family. The sitcom focuses on three couples: an older man, his younger Colombian wife and her son; a suburban couple with three children; and a gay couple with an adopted child.

BIG BANG!

One of TV's cleverest sitcoms is *The Big Bang Theory*, a show about a group of young scientists living near Los Angeles. A unique blend of science and humor, the sitcom stars Jim Parsons and Johnny Galecki as Sheldon Cooper and Leonard Hofstadter, physicists and roommates living across the hall from the beautiful Penny (played by Kaley Cuoco). Their nerdy friends Howard and Raj round out the cast in this witty sitcom playing on the rise of geek culture in America.

In this episode of *The Big Bang Theory*, Sheldon (*left*) builds a robotic copy of himself, which he remotely controls from his bedroom while his roommate, Leonard, has to drive said robot to work.

HEROES

Two of the decade's most successful science fiction shows were *Smallville* and *Heroes*. *Smallville*, on the CW, retold the Superman story from his teen years. Starring Tom Welling as young Clark Kent, the show fleshed out all the characters from the Superman serial and blended teenage angst with sci-fi special effects.

Like a comic book come to life, *Heroes* (2006–2010) featured everyday characters with various superpowers and spawned a lot of popular merchandise. Each character had a story arc focusing on the challenges of his or her powers, both personally and professionally.

DECADE IN REVIEW

Popular television in the first decade of the twenty-first century revealed a continued emphasis on reality programming, forensic dramas, and sitcoms. With the popularity of reality programs, the line between average citizen and professional celebrity has been redefined. Yet, the presence of well-written dramas also reveals the public's desire for more thoughtful entertainment. On this front, the culture was divided.

In 2011, Oprah Winfrey ended her daytime talk show, which had been on the air for twenty-five years—making Winfrey the most successful daytime talk show host in television history. Winfrey's show became a cultural phenomenon. Her focus on self-improvement and charity work earned many fans, and in her celebrity interviews were often noteworthy. Winfrey's daytime success made her one of the wealthiest and most powerful women in the world. After ending her talk show, Winfrey went on to host prime-time celebrity interviews and started her own cable channel—OWN—in 2011.

Television networks found new ways to deliver viewers their favorite programs. Most networks maintain their own websites—and many feature full episodes for viewing. The ser-

Perhaps no one person has had so much influence on so many people as Oprah Winfrey (*right*). Here she sits with President Barack Obama and First Lady Michelle Obama. Obama's successful candidacy was thought by many to have been helped in no small part by Oprah's championing of his bid.

vices Hulu, Netflix, and Amazon Instant Video, for example, allow subscribers to watch various programs at their own discretion by downloading or streaming full episodes or scenes.

With the success of these online services, some people in the television industry decided to eschew the traditional, but often slow, route of going through a television studio to get a show on the air, and created web series—shows that only air on the Internet—with writing and acting as high in quality as what one might find on television.

The first web series to find a large viewing audience was Joss Whedon's *Dr. Horrible's Sing-Along Blog*, which aired in 2008. It was created, written, shot, edited, and uploaded to Hulu during the Writer's Guild of America strike, which took place from November 5, 2007, to February 12, 2008, when the guild and the Alliance of Motion Picture and Television Producers reached an impasse regarding writers' royalty rights.

Starring Neil Patrick Harris, Felicia Day, and Nathan Fillion, *Dr. Horrible's Sing-Along Blog*, a musical tragicomedy about an aspiring supervillain trying to woo his dream girl, aired in three episodes on Hulu. *Dr. Horrible* became so beloved by fans and respected by critics and industry officials that it won several awards, including the number fifteen spot on *Time* magazine's "Top 50 Inventions of 2008" list and a Creative Arts Emmy for Outstanding Special Class—Short-format Live-Action Entertainment Programs.

After the success of *Dr. Horrible*, many other web series were launched, including *Misfits*, a British science fiction series only available to U.S. viewers online, and *The Guild*, created by *Dr. Horrible* alum Felicia Day, about a group of online gamers who try to cope with reality outside of their beloved game. Some writing teams of television series, like *Heroes*, *Battlestar Galactica*, and *The Walking Dead*, also embraced web-only content, and produced online-only episodes, called webisodes, that aired between episodes or provided back stories and supplemental information to the episodes that had already aired.

Social networking has also had a profound effect on television. In 2010, for example, a successful Facebook campaign led eighty-eight-year-old comedic actor Betty White to host *Saturday Night Live*. In 2012, YouTube announced that it would create dozens of channels featuring comedy, music, sports, and other forms of entertainment to compete with network and cable television.

By the 2011–2012 season, scripted shows appeared to be making a comeback—with more than twenty new dramas airing in the fall of 2011 and more in winter 2012. Still, the reality TV craze remained strong with a number of these programs still attracting large viewing audiences.

Conclusion

ARCHIE BUNKER'S CHAIR FROM THE 1970s sitcom
All in the Family is part of the permanent collection in the Smithsonian National Museum of American History in Washington, D.C. The threadbare chair where the fictional character sat represents a defining moment not only in the history of television, but also in the history of American popular culture.

That a sitcom could have such a powerful cultural impact illustrates the broad effect of popular television over the past sixty years. TV programs are a reflection of American life and culture. They depict changes in a culture and—because they reach so many people—they also influence culture in a variety of ways, from language to styles to attitudes to politics.

TV shows can also have a global reach, influencing other cultures. In 2011, plans were in place to translate the American sitcom *Everybody Loves Raymond* into versions in India, Israel, Egypt, and the Netherlands.

From dramas to sitcoms to reality shows, popular television continues to entertain world citizens and to comment on the human condition in new and insightful ways. Thanks to reruns, DVDs, and Internet downloading and streaming, the starship *Enterprise* continues its extraterrestrial journeys, Mary Richards still throws her hat into the air, and Ross still loves Rachel.

Ultimately, the history of popular television is a story of stories—many of which are yet to be told.

Notes

INTRODUCTION

p. 5, Statistics for percentages of television sets from Television History—the First 75 Years, www.tvhistory.tv/facts-stats.htm.

CHAPTER ONE

p. 9, "Popular shows included . . .": Harry Castleman and Walter J. Podrazik, *Watching TV: Six Decades of American Television*, 2nd ed. (Syracuse, NY: Syracuse University Press) 2010, 29.

p. 10, "America runs on . . .": Bulova company website. www.bulova.com/en_us/legacy.

CHAPTER TWO

p. 28, "*Captain Video* introduced . . .": SF Television website. www.magicdragon.com/UltimateSF/tv-chron.html.

p. 31, "Both shows . . .": Harry Castleman and Walter J. Podrazik, *Watching TV: Six Decades of American Television*, 2nd ed. (Syracuse, NY: Syracuse University Press) 2010, 145.

p. 35, "Although three Southern stations . . .": Castleman and Podrazik, 179.

p. 37, "More than 120 countries . . .": Jason Mitell, *Television and American Culture* (New York, Oxford: Oxford University Press) 2010, 395.

CHAPTER THREE

p. 42, "In January 1971 . . .": TV Party website. www.tvparty.com/70topten.html.

p. 44, "More than 100 million viewers . . .": *People: Television Shows That Changed Our Lives* (New York: People Books) 2010, 16.

p. 44, "Jump the Shark," Harry Castleman and Walter J. Podrazik, *Watching TV: Six Decades of American Television*, 2nd ed. (Syracuse, NY: Syracuse University Press) 2010, 270.

p. 45, "Seemed to power the era's culture . . .": Brooks Barnes, "Selling J.R., Lock, Stock and Swagger," *New York Times*, June 3, 2011. www.nytimes.com/2011/06/04/arts/television/larry-hagmans-dallas-memorabilia-on-auction-block.html.

CHAPTER FOUR

p. 53, "Whereas networks such as . . . ": Jason Mitell, *Television and American Culture* (New York, Oxford: Oxford University Press) 2010, 31.

p. 53, "By 1989, 60 . . . ": See Whitley, Peggy, "1980-1989," American Cultural History, Lone-Star College Kingwood library, 1999, kclibrary.lonestar.edu/decade80.html.

p. 55, "The show won Emmys . . ." TV Guide website. www.tvguide.com/tvshows/cosby/cast/100456.

p. 55, " . . . and some TV watchdogs . . .": Harry Castleman and Walter J. Podrazik, *Watching TV: Six Decades of American Television*, 2nd ed. (Syracuse, NY: Syracuse University Press) 2010, 334.

p. 62, "Hey, we are just like . . ." *The Simpsons Archive Round Springfield*, www.snpp.com/other/articles/roundspringfield.htm.

p. 64, "By 1989 . . . ""History of Cable TV Tips," Life Tips website. www.cabletv.lifetips.com/cat/64842/history-of-cable-tv/index.html.

CHAPTER FIVE

p. 74, "Is feminism dead? . . .": Ginia Bellafante, "Feminism: It's All About Me!", *TIME*, June 29, 1998. www.time.com/time/magazine/article/0,9171,988616,00.html.

CHAPTER SIX

p. 82, "Production costs for a reality program . . ." Jason Mitell, *Television and American Culture* (New York, Oxford: Oxford University Press) 2010, 86–87.

CONCLUSION

p. 98, "In 2011, plans were . . ." Sean Daly, "'Everybody Loves Raymond' Heading to Egypt, Israel, India." xfinitytv.comcast.net/blogs/2011/tv-news/everybody-loves-raymond-heading-to-israel-egypt-india/?cmpid=FCST_tvnews.

Further Information

BOOKS

Castleman, Harry, and Walter J. Podrazik. *Watching TV: Six Decades of American Television*. 2nd ed. Syracuse, NY: Syracuse University Press, 2010.

Durkee, Cutler, ed. *People: Television Shows That Changed Our Lives*. New York: People Books, 2010.

Mittell, Jason. *Television and American Culture*. New York, Oxford: Oxford University Press, 2010.

DVDS

The Golden Age of Television: The Criterion Collection. Criterion, 2009. Features performances of live television dramas from the 1950s.

Modern Marvels—Television: Window to the World. A & E Home Video, 2005. A history of television's effect on science, politics, culture, and social mores.

Pioneers of Television. PBS, 2005–2011. The series includes separate volumes on westerns, science fiction, children's programs, and crime drama.

WEBSITES

The History of Film, Television and Video
www.high-techproductions.com/historyoftelevision.htm
A year-by-year overview of advancements in television technology and programming, including a history of DVD and blu-ray, along with a store for videotape and disc products.

Hulu
www.hulu.com
Hulu is an online video service that offers episodes and clips from recent television shows, along with an extensive library of classic television shows. Shows can also be chosen by genre.

Most networks have their own website with information on programming, shows, and, often, full program episodes for viewing.

Television History—The First 75 Years.
www.tvhistory.tv/
A history of TV set design, development, and marketing. Includes "Quick Facts" by year, information on books and magazines, and a timeline.

Bibliography

Barnes, Brooks, "Selling J.R., Lock, Stock and Swagger," *New York Times*, June 3, 2011. www.nytimes.com/2011/06/04/arts/television /larry-hagmans-dallas-memorabilia-on-auction-block.html

Castleman, Harry, and Walter J. Podrazik. *Watching TV: Six Decades of American Television*. 2nd ed. Syracuse, NY: Syracuse University Press, 2010.

Daly, Sean, "'Everybody Loves Raymond' Heading to Egypt, Israel, India." July 29, 2011. Xfinity TV News. www.xfinitytv.comcast.net/ blogs/2011/tv-news/everybody-loves-raymond-heading-to-israel-egypt-india/?cmpid=FCST_tvnews

Durkee, Cutler, ed. *People: Television Shows That Changed Our Lives*. New York: People Books, 2010.

Mittell, Jason. *Television and American Culture*. New York, Oxford: Oxford University Press, 2010.

Pappademas, Alex. "The Year That TV Actually Got It Right." *The New York Times Magazine*. May 1, 2011.

Index

Page numbers in **boldface** are photographs.

The Adventures of Ozzie and Harriet, 12
The Adventures of Superman, 28, 30
advertising, 9, 10, 18, 88
affiliate stations, 53
Alias, 35
Alice, 69
All in the Family, 15, 40, 42, 50, 55, **63**, 99
Ally McBeal, 73–74
Amen, 56
American Bandstand, 18
An American Family, 45
American Idol, 6, 83–85, **84**
America's Got Talent, 85
Andy Griffith Show, 21, 26
The Andy Williams Show, 37
animation, 25, 34–35, 62, **63**, 79
The Apprentice, 85, 86
Arrested Development, 93
The Avengers, 35

Ball, Lucille, 13–14, **14**, 40
Barney Miller, 44
Batman, 30
Battlestar Galactica, 97
Baywatch, 64
Beatles, 22, 33, 37
Beauty and the Beast, 61

Ben Casey, 31
Berle, Milton, **8**, 10, 11
The Beverly Hillbillies, 26
Beverly Hills, 90210, 76
Bewitched, 26, 37
The Big Bang Theory, 94, **94**
Big Brother, 83
Big Love, 88
Bob Newhart Show, 44, 50
Bonanza, 21, 37, 40
Bones, 90
Boxing from Jamaica Arena, 9
The Brady Bunch, 27, 39
Broadway Preview, 9
Buffy the Vampire Slayer, 74, **75**
Burnett, Carol, 6, 11, 33, 40
Burns, George, 25, 64, 67

Cable Act of 1984, 53
cable TV, 53, 64, 79, 82–83, 86–90, **87**, **89**, 95
Cagney & Lacey, 58
Candid Camera, 82
Captain Video and His Video Rangers, 28
The Carol Burnett Show, 6, 11, 33, 50
catchphrases, 29, 34, 42, 44, 47, 69, 76, 86
Challenger blast, 51, **52**
Charlie's Angels, 40
Cheers, 54, 64, 67, 68

children's programming,
17, 18, 28–29, 35–37, **36**, 53
China Beach, 64
Civil Rights Act of 1964, 22
The Closer, 90
The Colbert Report, 79
Columbo, 47
COPS, 79
Cosby, Bill, 35, 54, 55
Cosby Show, 54–55, 64, 67
The Courtship of Eddie's Father, 37
CSI, 90
CSI: Miami, 90
CSI: New York, 90

The Daily Show with Jon Stewart,
78–79
Dallas, 46, 64
Dancing with the Stars, 85
Dateline NBC, 79
The Dating Game, 37
Dawson's Creek, 76
Deep Space Nine, 30
   See also *Star Trek*
Dennis the Menace, 18
Designing Women, 56
Desperate Housewives, 92
The Dick Van Dyke Show,
27, **27**, 28, **41**
A Different World, 56
Direct TV, 91
Doctor Who, 61
documentaries, 45
The Donna Reed Show, 18
downloading shows, 96, 99
Dragnet, 6, 47
drama series, 5, 9, 30, 40, 61, 74,
86, 98–99
   crime, 15, 31–32, 47, 58, **59**,
   70, **71**, 78, 90–91
   types of, 34–35, 45–46, 60, 73,
   77, 90–91, 94

dramedy, 56, 91–92
Dr. Horrible's Sing-Along Blog,
97
Dr. Kildare, 31
The Dukes of Hazzard, 50
Dynasty, 60–61

An Early Frost, 58
The Ed Sullivan Show, 10, **33**, 37
educational TV, 35–37, **36**, 45
Eight is Enough, 45
Ellen, 69
ensembles, 44, 54, 68, 90
ER, 31, 73, 91
Everybody Loves Raymond, 70, 99

Falcon Crest, 61
Family, 45
Family Guy, 25, 79
family hour, 45
Family Ties, 55
Fantasy Island, 50
Faraway Hill, 9
Father Knows Best, 12, 18, 40
FCC, 10, 45
feature films, 26, 28–30, **29**, 47,
   50, 73, 76, 86
Felicity, 76
feminism, 26, **41**, 42, 74
The Flintstones, 25
fourth wall, 25, 64
Frasier, 65, 68, 92
Friday Night Lights, 91
Friends, 6, 65, 68, 69
The Fugitive, 28, 60
Futurama, 79

game shows, 19, 37, 77–79, **78**
*The George Burns and Gracie
   Allen Show*, 25
Get Smart, 34
Gidget, 31

Gillette Cavalcade of Sports, 9
Gleason, Jackie, 15–16, **16**, 25
  See also *The Honeymooners*
Glee, 92
The Golden Girls, 54, 57, **57**, 64,
  67
Good Times, 40
Green Acres, 26
Grey's Anatomy, 31, 91
The Guild, 98
Gunsmoke, 40

hand-held camera, 58, 72
Happy Days, 44, 79
Have Gun—Will Travel, 17
Hawaiian Eye, 15
Hawaii Five-O, 47
Henson, Jim, **36**, 37
Hercules: The Legendary Journeys,
  74
Here's Lucy, 40
Heroes, 95
Hill Street Blues, 58, **59**
Hogan's Heroes, 37
homosexual, 40, 45, 69, 88
The Honeymooners, 15, **16**, 25,
  42, 55
  See also Gleason, Jackie
Honey West, 58
House M.D., 91
Howdy Doody, 17, 18
How I Met Your Mother, 68,
  93
Hullabaloo, 31

I Dream of Jeannie, 26
I Love Lucy, 6, 13–14, **14**, 44
  See also Ball, Lucille
In Living Color, 11, 56
Internet, **80**, 82, 85–86, 96–99,
  97
Ironside, 47

It's Garry Shandling's Show, 64
I've Got a Secret, 77

Jackie Gleason Show, 15
James Bond, 34
The Jeffersons, 40, 42
Jeopardy!, 77
The Jersey Shore, 69
The Jetsons, 25
Julia, 26

Kate and Allie, 56
Kennedy, John F., 21–22, **20**,
  37
Kent State, **38**, 39
kinescopes, 14
King of the Hill, 79
Knots Landing, 61
Kojak, 47
Kraft Television Theater, 9
Kukla, Fran and Ollie, 17

L.A. Law, 60, 64
laugh track, 56
Laverne & Shirley, 44
Law & Order, 58, **59**, 65, 70–72,
  71
Law & Order: Criminal Intent, 72
Law & Order: SVU, **71**, 72
Law & Order: UK, **71**, 72
Lawrence Welk Show, 37
Leave It to Beaver, 12, 13, 18, 39
Let's Make a Deal, 77
Life and Legend of Wyatt Earp,
  17
Little House on the Prairie, 45, 50
live broadcasting, 13
The Lone Ranger, 17
Lost in Space, 28–29, 69
Lou Grant, 40, 46
Love, American Style, 40
Love Boat, 50

Mad Men, 6, 83, 88–90, **89**

Man from U.N.C.L.E., 34

The Many Loves of Dobie Gillis, 25

Marcus Welby, M.D., 40

Married . . . with Children, 55

The Mary Tyler Moore Show, 13, 40–42, **41**, 46, 50, 54, 60

M*A*S*H, 40, 42, **43**, 44, 50

Maude, 40, 42

Maverick, 17

Mayberry RFD, 26, 37

Medium, 90

Melrose Place, 76

Miami Vice, 60

The Mickey Mouse Club, 17

Mission Impossible, 34, 47

Modern Family, 93

The Mod Squad, 31, **32**, 61

Monty Python's Flying Circus, 12

Moonlighting, 60

Moore, Mary Tyler, 13, 28, 41–42, **41**

Mork and Mindy, 50

Murder, She Wrote, 64

Murphy Brown, 54, 56, 58, 64, 67

music videos, 53, 56, 64, 92

My So-Called Life, 76

My Three Sons, 37

NCIS, 35, 90

network TV, 10, 53–55, 64, 70, 72–76, 79, 82, 95

Newhart, 54

The Newlywed Game, 37

news programming, 22, **38**, 39, 51–53, **52**, 66, **66**, 78, 79, 81, **81**

Nixon, Richard M., **20**, 21–22, 34, 39

Northern Exposure, 73

NYPD Blue, 58, 65, 70, 72

The Office, 93

One Day at a Time, 50

Our Miss Brooks, 13

Party of Five, 77

The Patty Duke Show, 31

Pee-wee's Playhouse, 18

Perry Mason, 15, 47

Petticoat Junction, 26

Peyton Place, 30

Police Woman, 58

political issues, 21–22, **20**, 37, 42, **49**, 49–50, 77

The Price Is Right, 19, 77

Private Secretary, 13

Quantum Leap, 61

racism, 35, 40, 42, 45, 66, 88, **89**

reality TV, 45–46, 78–79, **78**, 82–86, 94, 98, 99

The Real McCoys, 21

The Real World, 79

reruns, **14**, 30, 54, **71**, 99

Rhoda, 42

The Rifleman, 17

rock and roll, 22, 31, 33

Rocky and Bullwinkle Show, 34–35

Room 222, 40

Roseanne, 15, 54–55, 64, 67

Rowan & Martin's Laugh-In, 34, 37

Sanford and Son, 40

Saturday Night Live, 11–12, **49**, 93, 98

science fiction/fantasy, 23, **24**, 28–30, 61, 74–76, **75**, 94

Science Fiction Theatre, 28

Seinfeld, 65, 67, 69

selective service, 22

September 11, 2001, **80**, 81

Serling, Rod, 23, **24**

  See also *The Twilight Zone*

Sesame Street, 35–37, **36**

7ᵗʰ Heaven, 76

77 Sunset Strip, 15

Sex and the City, 83, 86, **87**

sexism, 12, 35, 88, **89**

Shindig!, 31

Simpson, O.J., 66, **66**

The Simpsons, 25, 62, **63**, 79

situation comedy (sitcom),
  5, 25, 50, 79

  as character-driven, 41–42, **41**,
   54, 86

  by decade, 12–**16**, 18, 21,
   26–28, 31–**32**, 37, 39–44, **48**,
   67–70, 92–94

  golden era (1980s), 54–58, **57**,
   62–64, **63**

$64,000 Question, 77

60 Minutes, 79

Smallville, 95

*The Smothers Brothers Comedy
  Hour*, 33–34, **33**, 37

Soap, 40

soap opera, 9, 30–31, 46, 60, 92

social issues, 23, **24**, 40, 45, 50,
 77

The Sopranos, 83, 86

South Park, 25, 79

So You Think You Can Dance, 85

Space Patrol, 28

space series, 28, 29, **29**

spinoff series, **29**, 30, 42, 46, 62,
  68, 72

*Sports from Madison Square
  Garden*, 9

Star Trek, 28–30, **29**, 74

Star Trek: The Next Generation,
  30, 61

Star Trek: Voyager, 74

St. Elsewhere, 31, 60, 91

streaming, 82, 96, 99

The Streets of San Francisco, 47

Sullivan, Ed, 10, 11, 22,
  33, 47

  See also *The Ed Sullivan Show,
   The Toast of the Town*

Survivor, 83

syndication, 74

Tales of Wells Fargo, 17

talk shows, 5, 95

Taxi, 44

technology, new, 51, **80**, 80–82,
  85–86, 99

teen-vampire genre, 74, **75**

television, impact of, 5–6

Texaco Star Theater, **8**, 10, 11

That Girl, 13, 26

That 70s Show, 79, 93

These Friends of Mine, 69

3ʳᵈ Rock from the Sun, 79

30 Rock, **27**, 93

Thirtysomething, 62

Three's Company, 40, 50

Till Death Us Do Part, 42

The Time Tunnel, 29

The Toast of the Town, 10, 11

  See also *The Ed Sullivan Show*

Tom Corbett-Space Cadet, 28

To Tell the Truth, 19

Twenty-One, 77

21 Jump Street, 61

20/20, 79

The Twilight Zone, 6, 23–25,
  24

Twin Peaks, 73, 75

Two and a Half Men, 92–93

227, 56

Ugly Betty, 92

The Untouchables, 47

variety programs, 10–12, 15, 19, 33–34, 40, 47–48, **48**, 56, 62

vaudeville, **8**, 11

Vietnam War, 22, 34, 42–43, **43**

Voyage to the Bottom of the Sea, 29

Wagon Train, 17

The Walking Dead, 97

Walt Disney Presents, 11, 23

Walt Disney's Wonderful World of Color, 23, 37

The Waltons, 45, 50, 62

web series, 97

Weeds, 88

westerns, 17, 21, 40, 61

The West Wing, 77

What's My Line, 19, 77

Wheel of Fortune, 77

The White Shadow, 50

Whose Line Is It Anyway?, 79

Who Wants to be a Millionaire, 77–78, **78**

Will & Grace, 65, 69–70, 92

Wilson, Flip, 47, **48**

Winfrey, Oprah, 95–96, **96**

The Wonder Years, 54, 55

writer's royalty rights, 97

Xena: Warrior Princess, 74

The X-Files, 65, 74, 76

The Young Riders, 61

Your Show of Shows, 12, 27